ELEANOR ROOSEVELT
First Lady

ELEANOR ROOSEVELT
First Lady

James T. Baker
Western Kentucky University

Harcourt Brace & Company

Fort Worth   Philadelphia   San Diego   New York   Orlando   Austin   San Antonio
Toronto   Montreal   London   Sydney   Tokyo

Publisher	Earl McPeek
Acquisitions Editor	David Tatom
Market Strategist	Steve Drummond
Developmental Editor	Margaret McAndrew Beasley
Project Editor	Angela Williams Urquhart
Art Director	Candice Johnson Clifford
Production Manager	Diane Gray

Cover and part-opening details: Douglas Chandor, *Eleanor Roosevelt.* White House Collection, White House Historical Association.

ISBN: 0-15-505704-9

Library of Congress Catalog Card Number: 98-87310

Address for Orders: Harcourt Brace College Publishers, 6277 Sea Harbor Drive, Orlando, FL 32887-6777, 1-800-782-4479

Address for Editorial Correspondence: Harcourt Brace College Publishers, 301 Commerce Street, Suite 3700, Fort Worth, TX 76102

Web Site Address: http://www.hbcollege.com

Printed in the United States of America

8 9 0 1 2 3 4 5 6 7   066   10 9 8 7 6 5 4 3 2 1

Harcourt Brace College Publishers

To my daughters Virginia and Elizabeth
—with hope for the future.

Eleanor Roosevelt: The most admired—and perhaps most criticized—woman of her times

> . . . *I must have a good deal of my uncle Theodore Roosevelt in me because I enjoy a good fight.* . . .
>
> ELEANOR ROOSEVELT
> *Autobiography*, 1958

> *Staying aloof is not a solution. It is a cowardly evasion.*
>
> ELEANOR ROOSEVELT
> *Tomorrow Is Now*, 1963

PREFACE

Eleanor Roosevelt: First Lady, the story of a turn-of-the-century American aristocrat who became First Lady of the United States and ultimately "First Lady of the World," is one in a series of books collectively called *Creators of the American Mind.*

ABOUT THE SERIES

Historians have noted that despite great diversity among the American people there is a collective American mind: a common way of thinking, molded by a common history, common hopes and dreams and by common fears. It is this mind that makes Americans a distinctive people. When Americans rally to constructive causes, the American mind gives them common conviction and focus. Even when they quarrel with one another, the American mind provides them with common subjects and ammunition for their arguments.

It is the thesis of this series of books that certain important individuals (political, social, religious, intellectual leaders, male and female, of all ethnic groups) have through their words and deeds helped create the American mind. Americans, whether they admire, despise, or fear these Creators, whether they even know of them, reflect in their own words and deeds the lives and accomplishments of these important persons. This series spotlights some of the Creators, listening when possible to their own words, comparing and contrasting the opinions and assessments of their biographers, juxtaposing their admirers and critics, all in an attempt to show what each one contributed to the American mind. Eleanor Roosevelt, the subject of this book, whatever one may think of her life and work, is certainly a Creator of the American Mind.

ABOUT THIS VOLUME

A daughter of wealth and social prominence, Eleanor Roosevelt married a distant cousin who gave her both joy and heartache and, by his election to the presidency, a chance to be First Lady of the United States. Through her own talents and courage she became the President's active partner in tackling the problems of Depression-era America and after his death earned the title, for her work at the United Nations, "First Lady of the World." This book offers a unique approach to the study of Eleanor Roosevelt. *Eleanor Roosevelt: First Lady*

- offers, under one cover, sufficient documents, with informative introductions, grouped logically and chronologically, for students to do research and writing on Eleanor Roosevelt's role as First Lady in Depression-era America and in World War II, as well as her work for civil rights and the American women's movement. It is comprehensive enough to cover these several topics fully, yet brief enough to serve as a supplementary reader in courses such as American History Survey, American Social and Intellectual History, and the History of American Women.
- presents her as a person (not an abstract character in a history book, but a real flesh-and-blood human being) by letting her speak for herself through her writings.
- places her in historical perspective by providing commentary on her life and work by friends who knew her and watched her at work and by scholars who have studied her life in depth. Students are provided an opportunity to judge the quality of personal testimony about and historians' analyses of an important public figure.
- shows her development as she grew from an early twentieth-century aristocrat (with a social conscience) to a revolutionary First Lady of the United States to her role in creating the United Nations, using her privileged positions to support civil rights and women's rights both at home and abroad.
- suggests, at appropriate intervals, questions that students may use to write responsive essays on the material.

- provides a list of topics for extended essays or term papers on Eleanor Roosevelt, the times in which she lived, and the work she did.
- includes an annotated bibliography so that students may dig deeper than this book can go into subjects suggested here.

Eleanor Roosevelt: First Lady demonstrates the power that an individual of talent, will, and opportunity can exert over the American republic. As she led the way in social, gender, and economic reform, first in the United States and later in the United Nations, she changed the way Americans thought on such issues as racial justice, concern for the weak and oppressed, and world peace. She helped create the American mind.

ACKNOWLEDGMENTS

The author is grateful to the following reviewers who read this book in manuscript form and offered constructive and corrective suggestions on how to make it a useful tool for classroom instruction: Stacy Cordery, Monmouth College; David Hamilton, University of Kentucky; Raymond Hyser, James Madison University; Michael Mayer, University of Montana; and Suzanne Marshall, Jacksonville State University.

Thanks also go to the Faculty Research Committee of Western Kentucky University, Elmer Gray, Chair, for funds to help bring the book to completion; to Elizabeth Jensen, who made the manuscript technically presentable; and to Drake Bush, David Tatom, Margaret Beasley, Angela Urquhart, Candice Clifford, and Diane Gray of Harcourt Brace College Publishers for their encouragement and expert advice.

CONTENTS

Part V
A WOMAN FIRST   153

CHRONOLOGY

"There is no such thing as being a bystander."

ELEANOR ROOSEVELT
The Moral Basis of Democracy, 1950

1884	Born October 11
1899–1902	Studied in England
1905	Married Franklin Roosevelt
1906	Daughter Anna born
1907	Son James born
1909	Son Franklin born and died
1910	Husband elected to the New York Legislature
	Son Elliott born
1913	Husband appointed Assistant Secretary of the Navy
1914	Son Franklin born
1916	Son John born
1918	Discovered her husband's infidelity
1920	Joined League of Women Voters
1921	Joined Women's Trade Union League
	Husband disabled by polio
1924–1928	Became active Democratic Party organizer
1928	Husband elected Governor of New York
1929–1933	First Lady of New York
1931	Formed close relationship with journalist Lorena Hickock
1932	Husband elected President of the United States
1933–1945	First Lady of the United States
1936	Began support of the American Student Union and Youth Congress
1938	Entertained King and Queen of Great Britain
1939	Resigned membership in the Daughters of the American Revolution; joined the National Association for the Advancement of Colored People
1941–1945	Active support of American efforts in World War II
1945	Husband died
	Appointed American representative to the United Nations by President Harry Truman, delegate 1945–1953

1948   Oversaw passage of the United Nations' Declaration on
            Human Rights
            Supported Truman's candidacy in presidential election
1961   Chaired President John F. Kennedy's Commission on the
            Status of Women
1962   Died November 7 of complications resulting from a rare
            form of bone-marrow tuberculosis

INTRODUCTION

Long ago, there was a noble word, liberal, *which derives from the word* free. . . . *We must cherish the word free or it will cease to apply to us.*

ELEANOR ROOSEVELT
Tomorrow Is Now, 1963

. . . while an indestructible faith in human decency and possibility was the center of her life, all this was accompanied by an impressive capacity for salty realism and, on occasion, for a kind of quasi-gentle mercilessness.

ARTHUR SCHLESINGER, JR.
Foreword to *Eleanor and Franklin,* 1971

Among the most influential persons of the twentieth century was Eleanor Roosevelt, who was First Lady (wife of the President) of the United States from 1933 to 1945. From the time her husband, Franklin Delano Roosevelt (FDR), was elected Governor of New York in 1928, and even more after he was elected President of the United States in 1932, Eleanor Roosevelt (ER) was a remarkable, revolutionary, unforgettable public figure in her own right. While in the White House she was an outspoken advocate of social, racial, and economic justice and of equal rights and opportunities for women and minorities. After FDR's death in 1945 she became an equally active advocate for such human rights around the world. Using her prominence, taking full advantage of national and world events, speaking to audiences in person and through print, radio, and finally television, ER molded American opinion on every vital issue of her day. She must certainly be included in the front ranks of those we recognize as Creators of the American Mind.

As a result of her outspoken and highly visible role in the causes she embraced, she was at the same time one of the most admired and most criticized public figures of the twentieth century. Her admirers praised this new kind of First Lady, one who spoke for the poor, for minorities, for women, for youth, as a veritable godsend to a nation in desperate need of reform. Her critics, among them conservative-to-reactionary politicians and pundits, considered her naive, probably dangerous, and they labeled her "do-goodism" a sure sign of the nation's decline. The conservative columnist Westbrook Pegler, who never overlooked an opportunity to lampoon her liberalism, dubbed her "La Boca Grande," which is Spanish for "The Big Mouth."

These contradictory assessments of her activism continued long after she left the White House—to her death and even beyond. The two articles that follow, written soon after she died, are typical of the two opinions of her life and work. The first, "Eleanor Roosevelt: A Lady for All Seasons," appeared in *Saturday Review* in 1964, when she would have been eighty years old. It was written by her admirer Adlai Stevenson, a liberal Democrat whom Eleanor had twice supported for President, in 1952 and in 1956. In 1964 Stevenson was U.S. Ambassador to the United Nations, serving under President Lyndon Johnson, whose domestic program called The Great Society was patterned after FDR's domestic program, the New Deal.

Stevenson uses both political and religious language to establish ER as a central figure, a force for good, in modern American public affairs. Notice how he uses her continuing moral influence to support the Johnsonian policies of reform at home and opposition to aggression abroad.

Eleanor Roosevelt was a lady—a lady for all seasons. Like her husband, she left "a name to shine on the entablatures of truth—forever."

It is hard to condense what one can say about this remarkable, brave, warm, practical, and persistent woman who gave herself to her time as no one else in her generation. However, in remembering her on what would have been her eightieth birthday, what comes to mind first is the fact that in nearly fourscore years she never ran out of things that needed doing, and she worked all her days for the realization of a human city embracing all mankind.

When she died on that gray November day in 1962, she was the most respected woman of this century. Some small measure of that respect was evidenced in the score of eulogies delivered in the General Assembly of the United Nations—the first and only time a private citizen was so honored. I recalled then that she gave her faith not only to those who shared the privilege of knowing her and of working by her side, but to countless men, women, and children in every part of the globe who loved her even as she loved them.

* * *

I do not suggest some unworldly saint dwelling in remote regions of unsullied idealism. On the contrary, as we all know, Eleanor Roosevelt was a bonny fighter, at her best down in the arena, face to face with opponents and ideas she disapproved, and in ripe old age she took on tasks that might have daunted people half her age.

Whether it was Communist bosses in the United Nations where she was the inspired architect of the Declaration of Human Rights, whether it was shoddy politicians, whether it was exploiters of the poor or traducers of the faith of freedom no matter where—she sailed in, tall, courteous, good-tempered, implacable, and thwacked them with the dispassionate energy of a good mother chastising a bad boy.

She was a remarkable person, this great and gallant woman who was known as the First Lady of the World. She was strong but gentle, idealistic but practical, humble as well as proud. She thought of herself as an "ugly duckling," but she walked in beauty in the slums and ghettos of the world, bringing with her the reminder of her beloved St. Francis, ". . . it is in the giving that we receive. . . ." And where ever she walked beauty was forever there.

* * *

So, though she has left us—our counselor, our friend, our conscience—there can be no doubt where she would be directing our efforts today.

She would bid us add to the equality we now guarantee by law the extra dimension of opportunity without which even important rights can seem so much emptiness.

She would counsel us that we have done no more than set the framework within which the real struggle must still be fought out.

She would tell us to look at our great cities and ask ourselves whether, in the midst of overwhelming affluence, we can afford such misery, such squalor, such haplessness.

She would tell us to labor on in the vineyards of the world, to succor the needy, to underpin the rule of law, to check aggression, and, with remorseless purpose, to seek peace among nations.

She would ask us to engage ourselves profoundly in the war on poverty at home and abroad.

She would urge us to build the great society not only for America, but for all God's children, so that all people everywhere are henceforth considered equal in dignity, equal in responsibility, equal in self-respect.

She did her share, more than any of us can do, to turn magnificent promises into even more magnificent facts—facts we must now and ever defend against those in our society who would like to escape history, to evade the fiery trial, to turn back the clock. Eleanor Roosevelt never would and never did.

She had the courage to battle everlastingly for something better and the prescience to "see a world in a grain of sand, and a Heaven in a wild flower." Happily for us, she could share her dream of a better tomorrow with all of us. That was, of course, the key to her greatness, the very reason of her life.

And we will fulfill the rich legacy she has left us only to the extent we make real her dream and press forward even as she in the patient, unspectacular, lonely search for the interests that unite the nations and toward the ultimate victory of reason, racial harmony, and justice in a world ruled by law.

And what finer remembrance could there be for Eleanor Roosevelt?

The mirror opposite of Stevenson's celebratory eulogy is the following commentary by William F. Buckley, conservative writer and publisher, who considered Eleanor Roosevelt not only a meddler in affairs she did not understand but an out-and-out threat to America's future well-being. The following article, "Mrs. Roosevelt: RIP," appeared in Buckley's *National Review*. Although Buckley was among the few commentators with the courage or temerity to ridicule ER at the time of her death, he probably represented the opinion of a sizable minority of Americans who hoped ER's influences would wane.

I have been sharply reminded that I have not written about Mrs. Roosevelt, and that only a coward would use the excuse that when she died, he was in Africa. There, there are lions and tigers and apartheid. Here, there was Mrs. Roosevelt to write about. Africa was the safer place.

People get very sore when you knock the old lady. And it isn't just the widow who thinks of Mrs. Roosevelt as the goddess who saved her children from getting rickets during the Depression. It is also the Left-intellectuals. "When are you going to stop picking on Mrs. Roosevelt?" a very learned writer asked me at a reception a few years ago after one of my books was published. (I had a sentence in it that annoyed him, something like, "Following Mrs. Roosevelt in search of irrationality is like following a lighted fuse in search of an explosion: one never has to wait very long.") I answered: "When you begin picking on her." I meant by that that people are best reformed by those they will listen to. Westbrook Pegler could never reform Mrs. Roosevelt, or her legend. But Adlai Stevenson, or Max Lerner, might have.

The obituary notices on Mrs. Roosevelt were as one in granting her desire to do good—she treated all the world as her own personal slum project: and all papers, of course, remarked on that fabulous energy—surely she was the very first example of the peacetime use of atomic energy. But some publications (I think especially of *Times*) went so far as to say she had a great mind. Now is the time for all good men to come to the aid of Euclid.

Does it matter? Alas, it happens to matter very much. For Mrs. Roosevelt stamped upon her age a mode. Or, it might be said by those who prefer to put it that way, that in Mrs. Roosevelt the age developed its perfect symbol. Hers is the age of undifferentiated goodness, of permissive egalitarianism.

Mrs. Roosevelt's approach to human problems, so charming in its Franciscan naivete, was simply: do away with them—by the most obvious means. The way to cope with Russia is to negotiate. . . . The way for everyone to be free in the world is to tell the UN to free everyone. . . . The way to solve the housing shortage is for the government to build more houses. . . .

All that is more than Mrs. Roosevelt writing a column. It is a way of life. Based, essentially, on unreason; on the leaving out of the concrete, complex factor, which is why they call it "undifferentiated" goodness. Negotiation with Russia, you see, implies there is something we are, or should be, prepared to yield. . . . And everyone in the world cannot be free so long as freedoms are used by whole nations to abuse the peoples of other nations or the freedoms of their own people. . . . Latin American poverty is something that grows out of the pores of Latin American institutions and appetites, and cannot be seriously ameliorated by mere transfusions of American cash. . . . And the way to get houses built is to reduce their cost, so poor people can buy them, without paying crippling wages to monopoly labor unions, or crippling prices to manufacturing concerns that have to pay the taxes of a government which among other things decides it needs to get into the housing business. . . .

Mrs. Roosevelt's principal bequest, her most enduring bequest, was the capacity so to oversimplify problems as to give encouragement to those who wish to pitch the nation and the world onto humanitarian crusades which, because they fail to take reality into account, end up plunging people into misery (as Wilson's idealistic imperialism plunged Europe into misery for several years, and spawned Hitler), and messing up the world in general (under whose statecraft did Stalin prosper?). Above all it was Mrs. Roosevelt who, on account of her passion for the non sequitur, deeply wounded the processes of purposive political thought. "Over whatever subject, plan, or issue Mrs. Roosevelt touches," Professor James Burnham once wrote, "she spreads a squidlike ink of directionless feeling. All distinctions are blurred, all analysis fouled, and in the murk clear thought is forever impossible."

Some day in the future, a Liberal scholar will write a definitive thesis exploring the cast of Mrs. Roosevelt's mind by a textual analysis of her thought: and then history will be able to distinguish between a great woman with a great heart, and a woman of perilous intellectual habit. "With all my heart and soul," her epitaph should read. "I fought the syllogism." And with that energy and force, she wounded it, almost irretrievably—how often have you seen the syllogism checking in at the office for a full day's work lately?

These two assessments show that no one who knew Eleanor Roosevelt held a moderate opinion of her. Everyone felt strongly one way or the other about her. Whether she was a humanitarian reformer who made positive contributions to her country and the world or was a shallow busybody who meddled in matters she did not understand and made things worse depends on the philosophy and perspective of the observer. No one denied that she was a persistent, unflappable, and effective spokesperson for the causes she espoused.

This is the story of how Eleanor Roosevelt, an aristocratic "lady" of early twentieth-century America, became a public woman; of how she permanently changed the role of First Lady of the United States; and of how she helped shape the modern world. While I confess that I am one of those who applaud her contributions to social reform, to economic, racial, and sexual justice, I hope to tell her story with sufficient objectivity that you can judge her for yourself. One thing you will likely decide, as have all of her admirers and critics alike, is that neither women, First Ladies, the United States, nor the world have been quite the same since Eleanor Roosevelt played her scenes on the stage of history. No one deserves more than she to be called a Creator of the American mind.

ELEANOR ROOSEVELT

First Lady

PART I

The Formation of a Public Woman

About the only value the story of my life may have is to show that one can, even without any particular gifts, overcome obstacles that seem insurmountable.

—ELEANOR ROOSEVELT
Autobiography, 1961

Both by fate and personal will, Eleanor Roosevelt became the most important public woman of the twentieth century. . . . Yet behind her public image lay a private personality tormented by the quest for emotional support, warmth, and intimacy.

—WILLIAM H. CHAFE
Without Precedent, 1984

YOUTH, EDUCATION, MARRIAGE, AND MOTHERHOOD (1884–1918), AS TOLD BY DORIS KEARNS GOODWIN, HELEN DOUGLAS, AND ELEANOR ROOSEVELT HERSELF

Eleanor Roosevelt was born into a New York family of Dutch descent that enjoyed great wealth and social prominence; she was by birth an American aristocrat; yet she experienced a singularly unhappy childhood. During the first fifteen years of her life, as she was taught to live by the standards of her day and social class, she developed feelings of inferiority that not even a successful time at school or her marriage to an attractive, successful man ever erased. She continued for the remainder of her life to doubt herself and had constantly to fight a stubborn timidity.

The story of ER's early years of anguish is best told by Doris Kearns Goodwin. Goodwin, a respected historian who has written biographies of President Lyndon Johnson and the family of President John Kennedy, included the following account of ER's childhood for her book on Franklin and Eleanor Roosevelt, *No Ordinary Time*. She begins by describing ER's parents, the tragic Elliott and Anna, and how their troubles affected ER:

> Elliott Roosevelt and Anna Hall made a dazzling couple. They were invited everywhere, and Anna fell in love. Like so many others, she, too, was affected by Elliott's radiant smile and charming personality. She was nineteen and he was twenty-three when they married. Their happiness was short-lived. The responsibility of marriage and the birth of three children—Eleanor, Elliott Jr., and Hall—served to increase Elliott's anxiety to the point where his casual drinking became heavier and heavier.
>
> When he was not drinking, he was loving and warm, everything Eleanor wanted in a father. "[My father] dominated my life as long as he lived and was the love of my life for many years after he died," Eleanor wrote in her memoirs. One of her earliest recollections is of being dressed up and allowed to come down and dance for a group of her father's friends, who enthusiastically applauded her performance. Then, when she finished, her father would pick her up and hold her high in the air, a moment of triumph for both the father and the little girl. "With my father I was perfectly happy," she recalled. "He would take me into his dressing room in the mornings or when he was dressing for dinner and let me watch each thing he did."
>
> When he was drinking, however, everything changed. The routine of everyday life became impossible to maintain. The household was filled with recrimination. Night after night he would show up too late for dinner, and many nights he failed to show up at all. At one point, he made a servant girl pregnant and a scandal erupted in the newspapers. At times, his drinking led to a melancholy so deep that he threatened suicide. In such moods, he would totally forget the promises he had made to his wife and his daughter only the day before. One afternoon, Eleanor recalled, her father took her and three of their dogs for a walk. As they

came up to the door of the Knickerbocker Club,[1] he told Eleanor to wait for a moment with the dogs and he would be right back. An hour passed, and then another, and then four more, and still Eleanor remained at the door, patiently holding the dogs. Finally, her father came out, but so drunk that he had to be carried in the arms of several men. The doorman took Eleanor home.

Still, Eleanor preferred her warm and affectionate father to her cold and self-absorbed mother. At least with her father, she said, she never doubted that she "stood first in his heart," whereas for as long as she could remember she felt that her beautiful mother was bitterly disappointed, almost repelled, by the plainness and the ungainliness of her only daughter. Forced to wear a brace for several years for curvature of the spine, Eleanor recalled that even at the age of two she was "a shy solemn child," completely "lacking in the spontaneous joy or mirth of youth." Moreover, she knew, "as a child senses those things," that her mother was trying to compensate for her lack of beauty by teaching her excellent manners, but "her efforts only made me more keenly conscious of my shortcomings."

Perhaps Anna, having been taught to value beauty and charm as the most important attributes in a woman, did instinctively recoil from her daughter's unattractive looks. But, though Eleanor could never admit it, her father's erratic behavior was the more likely cause of the distance between mother and daughter. Feeling the weight of the world on her shoulders, Anna had little energy left for a stubborn and precocious little girl who kept her father on a pedestal and blamed her mother when her father had to be sent away on various "cures" to various sanitariums. Perhaps, in rejecting Eleanor's fervent love for her father, Anna was rejecting that part of herself that had fallen in love with such an untrustworthy man.

Eleanor slept in her mother's room while her father was away and could hear her mother talking with her aunts about the problem with her father. "I acquired a strange and garbled idea of the troubles which were going on around me. Something was wrong with my father." Eleanor was only seven at the time, too young to understand the intolerable strain on her twenty-eight-year-old mother, a strain that produced in Anna very bad recurring headaches. "I would sit at the head of her bed and stroke her head,"

---

[1] A private club for wealthy and socially prominent New York men. Eleanor's father was a member.

Eleanor recalled. "The feeling that I was useful was perhaps the greatest joy I had experienced."

But aside from these dreamy moments serving her mother, Eleanor felt most of the time "a curious barrier" between herself and the rest of her little family. In the late afternoons, she recalled, her mother sat in the parlor with her two brothers. "Little Ellie adored her, the baby [Hall] sat on her lap. . . . [I can] still remember standing in the door, very often with my finger in my mouth —which was, of course, forbidden and I can see the look in her eyes and hear the tone of her voice as she said, 'Come in, Granny.' If a visitor was there she might turn and say: 'She is such a funny child, so old-fashioned, we always call her Granny.' I wanted to sink through the floor in shame, and I felt I was apart from the boys." The painful memory of these afternoons in the parlor remained with Eleanor, reappearing thirty years later in fictional composition in which she wrote of "a blue eyed rather ugly little girl standing in the door of a cozy library looking in at a very beautiful woman holding, oh so lovingly, in her lap a little fair haired boy."

For most of Eleanor's eighth year, her father remained in exile in Abingdon, Virginia,[2] where her mother and her uncle Theodore had sent him in the hope that the forced separation from his family would motivate him to take hold of himself. "A child stood at a window . . . ," Eleanor wrote in her composition book. "Her father [was] the only person in the world she loved, others called her hard & cold but to him she was everything lavishing on him all the quiet love which the others could not understand. And now he had gone she did not know for how long but he had said 'what ever happens little girl some day I will come back' & she had smiled. He never knew what the smile cost."

On her eighth birthday, Eleanor received a long and loving letter from Abingdon, addressed to "My darling little Daughter." "Because Father is not with you is not because he doesn't love you," he wrote. "For I love you tenderly and dearly. And maybe soon I'll come back all well and strong and we will have such good times together, like we used to have. I have to tell all the little children here often about you and all that I remember of you when you were a little bit of a girl and you used to call yourself Father's little 'Golden Hair'—and how you used to come into my dressing room and dress me in the morning and frighten me by saying I'd be late for breakfast."

---

[2] Elliott agreed to live there and work for a relative in order to give his family a respite from his erratic behavior.

These letters, filled only with love for her, Eleanor later wrote, were the letters she loved and kissed before she went to bed. But there were other letters, filled with news of the life he was leading in Abingdon, that inadvertently brought her pain and reinforced her feeling of being an outsider. In these newsy letters he often spoke of riding horseback with a group of little children near where he lived. "I was always longing to join the group," Eleanor later wrote. "One child in particular I remember. I envied her very much because he was so very fond of her."

A month after Eleanor's eighth birthday, her mother contracted a fatal case of diphtheria.[3] Her father was told to return from his exile in Virginia, but Anna died before he was able to get home. "I can remember standing by a window when Cousin Susie told me that my mother was dead," Eleanor later wrote. "Death meant nothing to me, and one fact wiped out everything else—my father was back and I would see him very soon."

When Elliott finally arrived, Eleanor recorded, "he held out his arms and gathered me to him. In a little while he began to talk, to explain to me that my mother was gone, that she had been all the world to him and now he only had my brothers and myself, that my brothers were very young and that he and I must keep close together. Some day I would make a home for him again, we would travel together and do many things. Somehow it was always he and I. I did not understand whether my brothers were to be our children or whether he felt that they would be at school and college and later independent. There started that day a feeling which never left me that he and I were very close together and some day would have a life of our own together. . . . When he left, I was all alone to keep our secret of mutual understanding."

The decision was made to send Eleanor and her brothers to their grandmother Hall's while Elliott returned to Virginia. From then on, Eleanor admitted, "subconsciously I must have been waiting always for his visits. They were irregular and he rarely sent word before he arrived, but never was I in the house even in my room two long flights of stairs above the entrance door that I did not hear his voice the minute he entered the front door." During these precious visits, Elliott painted a picture for his daughter of the valiant, gifted, upright little girl he expected her to be, and Eleanor did her best, she later wrote, despite her consciousness of her ugly looks and her many deficiencies, to make herself into "a fairly good copy of the picture he had painted."

---

[3] An acute infectious disease that affects the respiratory system and in these days often proved fatal.

The year after her mother died Eleanor's four-year-old brother, Ellie, also fell ill with diphtheria and died. Though she was a child herself, Eleanor tried to comfort her father. "We must remember," she wrote him, "Ellie is going to be safe in heaven and to be with Mother who is waiting there. . . . "

But then, when Eleanor was ten, the visits and the letters from her father stopped. The years of heavy drinking took their final toll. Suffering from delirium tremens,[4] Elliott tried to jump out of the window of his house, had a seizure and died, at the age of thirty-four. "My aunts told me," Eleanor recalled, "but I simply refused to believe it, and while I wept long . . . I finally went to sleep and began the next day living in my dream world as usual. My grandmother decided we children should not go to the funeral and so I had no tangible thing to make death real to me. From that time on . . . I lived with him more closely, probably, than I had when he was alive."

From the melancholy lives of both her parents, as she would learn again in her own marriage, Eleanor had come to understand that promises were made to be broken, and that no one's love for her was meant to last. The legacy of repeated loss as a child left her prey to the recurring depressions she suffered as an adult. Always waiting in the wings, depression was for Eleanor a dark companion that strode to center stage whenever there were turn-abouts in the established pattern of her life.

✳ ✳ ✳

But the legacy of Eleanor's childhood also produced resilient strength. No matter how many times her father disappointed her, Eleanor knew, at bottom, that he loved her profoundly, that he had chosen her as his favorite child. And this knowledge was something that neither alcoholism nor death could destroy. "It was her father who acquainted Eleanor with grief," Joe Lash[5] has written. "But he also gave her the ideals that she tried to live up to all her life by presenting her with the picture of what he wanted her to be—noble, studious, religious, loving and good."

"We do not have to become heroes overnight," Eleanor once wrote. "Just a step at a time, meeting each thing that comes up, seeing it is not as dreadful as it appears, discovering that we have the strength to stare it down." So, step by step, Eleanor willed her-

---

[4] A condition caused by excessive alcoholic consumption typified by extreme agitation and often hallucinations.

[5] More about Lash later.

self to become the accomplished daughter her father had decreed her to be, the fearless woman that would make him proud. Every inch of her journey was filled with peril and anxiety, but she never stopped moving forward. "The thing always to remember," she said, is that "you must do the thing you think you cannot do."

ER's life then was marked forever by the loss of her glamorous but tragic parents. She had to reach adulthood without her mother's beauty or her father's love. This made her both insecure and determined. Had she not known so much pain, she might well not have known so much success. Her closest friends and political allies recognized the impact her early sorrows had on her. Helen Gahagan Douglas, a film actor and then a liberal California Congresswoman who had opportunity to share not only political causes but also many intimate moments with ER while she was First Lady, recalled in her book *The Eleanor Roosevelt We Remember* the following poignant comments Eleanor made about those painful early years of her life, particularly her feelings of unattractiveness:

> In one of her very last interviews, Mrs. Roosevelt reminded us that she grew up as the "ugly duckling" in a family of beautiful people.
> She said, speaking of her family, "They were all very great social successes. . . . A woman with the background we grew up in was educated in order to be a success in society. You learned languages. If you were fortunate enough to be able to play the piano or sing a little bit, that was very pleasant, but everything you did was so that you would grace society. . . . To be a beautiful woman would be an enormous asset, and all of my mother's family were beautiful, and so it was a shock to the family when I was just a very ordinary looking little girl. . . . "
> Again speaking of her lack of beauty, she said, "You tried to make up for it by being well educated and having very good manners, and, well, you tried to follow the code, and the code of my grandmother was that whenever you were expected to do something in a social way, you did it and you didn't say, 'I have a headache and I'm not going to go to this party,' you went and you were as agreeable as you could be."

The "ugly duckling" Eleanor Roosevelt, like the one in the original children's story, determined that she would in every possible way grow up to be a lovely swan. She would fulfill her father's expectations. She would live according to her grandmother Hall's social code of duty. That code made certain demands. She must be properly educated. Her schools were all private, and they taught subjects that young aristocratic women needed to know: subjects designed to make them charming wives and mothers. In 1899, after attending local schools, ER's grandmother sent her to England, to a boarding school (often referred to as a "finishing" school) near London called Allenswood. There she came under the tutelage of the seventy-year-old French-born headmistress, a woman named Marie Souvestre, who for three years taught her French and history, showing respect for ER's mind, and treated her as her own child. In Mlle. Souvestre she found, rather late for her psychological well-being, the maternal love that had been so lacking in her childhood; and she later wrote, "Whatever I have become since had its seed in those three years of contact with [her] liberal mind and strong personality."

Mlle. Souvestre more than once took ER with her when she visited the European continent during summer holidays. ER later recalled those holiday journeys:

> As I think back over my trips with Mlle. Souvestre, I realize she taught me how to enjoy traveling. She liked to be comfortable, she enjoyed good food, but she always tried to go where you would see the people of the country you were visiting, not your own compatriots.
>
> She always ate native dishes and drank native wines. She felt it was just as important to enjoy good Italian food as it was to enjoy Italian art, and it all served to make you a citizen of the world, at home wherever you might go, knowing what to see and what to enjoy. She used to impress on my mind the necessity for acquiring languages, primarily because of the enjoyment you missed in a country when you were both deaf and dumb.
>
> Mlle. Souvestre taught me also on these journeys that the way to make young people responsible is to throw real responsibility on them. She was an old lady and I was sixteen. The packing and unpacking for both of us was up to me, once we were on the road. I looked up trains, got the tickets, made all the detailed arrangements necessary for comfortable traveling. Though I was to lose some of my self-confidence and ability to look after myself

in the early days of my marriage, it came back to me later more easily because of these trips with Mlle. Souvestre.

At Allenswood School, ER started what was for her "a new life." There for the first time she blossomed as a person. She excelled in all her studies and placed high in school contests, everything from poetry reading to field hockey. Her three years there, she said, "were the happiest of my life." She left for home in 1902 with regret:

The summer was now approaching, and I knew that I must go home for good. Mlle. Souvestre had become one of the people whom I cared most for in the world, and the thought of the long separation seemed hard to bear. I would have given a good deal to have spent another year on my education, but to my grandmother the age of eighteen was the time when you "came out,"[6] and not to "come out" was unthinkable.

When I left I felt quite sure that I would return before long, but I realize now that Mlle. Souvestre, knowing her infirmities, had little hope of seeing me again. She wrote me lovely letters, which I still cherish. They show the kind of relationship that had grown up between us and give an idea of the fine person who exerted the greatest influence, after my father, on this period of my life.

A second expectation for a young woman of ER's class was that she use her education to make a good marriage and serve as a faithful wife and effective mother. But back in the United States, where her uncle Theodore Roosevelt was the President, while she dutifully "came out," she showed signs of being one of those "new" American women who preferred social work among society's unfortunate classes to the parties and balls where proper young women met proper young men. In the Progressive spirit of the times, she volunteered to teach the children of recent immigrants in the Rivington Settlement House in New York City, one of hundreds such centers designed to teach needy boys and girls the values of their adopted country and the skills needed to succeed in it. She specialized in teaching boys to dance.

---

[6] To "come out" for young women of the New York elite meant to be presented to society, usually through a fancy ball. It was also an announcement that the young woman was of marriageable age.

Although she generally avoided social events, she did manage to make friends with a young man, one of her distant cousins, whom she had known in childhood but had not seen for many years, Franklin Delano Roosevelt. FDR was a handsome and dashing (if a bit shallow) Harvard student; but he found his somewhat "plain" cousin Eleanor intriguing. Unlike most of the girls he knew, she was serious and intelligent, could talk of history and philosophy, and found debutante balls frivolous. He invited her to Harvard football games and to his mother's estate at Hyde Park, where they rode horses together and read poetry to each other. He learned from her things he would not have learned elsewhere. Once when he picked her up at Rivington for a date, she introduced him to a world his wealthy, sheltered life had not prepared him to see. "My god," he said when they were away from the Settlement House, "I didn't know anyone lived like that." It was only the first of many ways of life, so different from his own life of privilege and ease, that she would force him to face and help him understand.

ER as society woman and wife to the aspiring young lawyer, Franklin Delano Roosevelt

They fell in love. When after a year's courtship he proclaimed his love and asked her to marry him, she recalled, "I did not hesitate to say yes, for I knew I loved him too." They married in 1905, when he graduated from Harvard. Her Uncle Theodore, having just been elected to his own term as President of the United States, gave the bride away. She told friends in those days that she was blissfully happy with FDR and believed she would always be so. But when in old age she wrote her autobiography, she described that time in her life with a more balanced judgment. Troubles she could not see in 1905 were easy to see half a century later. After a forty-year marriage, filled with children, illness, success, and betrayal, she saw her newly married self clearly:

> I had painfully high ideals and a tremendous sense of duty entirely unrelieved by any sense of humor or any appreciation of the weaknesses of human nature. Things were either right or wrong to me, and I had had too little experience to know how fallible human judgments are.
>
> I had a great curiosity about life and a desire to participate in every experience that might be the lot of a woman. There seemed to me to be a necessity for hurry; without rhyme or reason I felt the urge to be a part of the stream of life, and so in the autumn of 1903, when Franklin Roosevelt, my fifth cousin once removed, asked me to marry him, though I was only nineteen, it seemed entirely natural and I never even thought that we were both young and inexperienced. I came back from Groton, where I had spent the weekend, and asked Cousin Susie whether she thought I cared enough, and my grandmother, when I told her, asked me if I was sure I was really in love. I solemnly answered "yes," and yet I know now that it was years later before I understood what being in love or what loving really meant.
>
> I had high standards of what a wife and mother should be and not the faintest notion of what it meant to be either a wife or a mother, and none of my elders enlightened me. I marvel now at my husband's patience, for I realize how trying I must have been in many ways. I can see today how funny were some of the tragedies of our early married life.

ER played the role of "lady" with the same determination she demonstrated throughout her life. She got married, gave birth to six children (one of whom died in infancy), and was a "good wife" who encouraged FDR as he finished law school and started a law practice in New York City. All these things were complicated by the constant presence of her mother-in-law, Sara Delano Roosevelt. Long a widow, Sara had raised her only son to be a "mama's boy,"[7] and she had no intention of allowing marriage to take him away from her. A woman of fierce will, she had not particularly approved Franklin's choice of ER as his wife (some of her friends believed she feared the Elliott Roosevelt weaknesses might be transferable to ER); and she was determined to keep the young couple and their children under her control. Everywhere they lived during their early married life, Sara lived nearby, sometimes in an adjoining apartment. Always she directed their affairs and gave ER orders. She even told ER's children that while ER "bore" them, she was their true mother.

ER was happy when Franklin ran successfully for the New York State Legislature, being elected from a Dutchess County district that had always been Republican. But she found her role as a politician's wife, with its teas and balls, almost as difficult as life under Sara. It was even worse when in 1913 FDR was named Assistant Secretary of the Navy by Democratic President Woodrow Wilson. Washington was just more public affairs without real purpose. But she played her role through the years of World War I, attending rallies and parties, but finding peace and happiness only during holidays at the family retreat on Campobello Island in the Bay of Fundy. Campobello, off the coast of Maine, is Canadian soil but had appeal for many Americans.

Then in 1918, the year that the war ended, something happened that changed ER's married life forever, something so painful that, as she later wrote "the bottom dropped out of my own particular world." It was then that she discovered a love affair between her husband and her social secretary, Lucy Page Mercer.

When she found their love letters, she fell into despair and remained despondent for many months. When she emerged from this second dark valley of her life, she was a stronger woman than she had been before entering it. "I really grew up that year," she later wrote about the affair without ever revealing what it was. She found the grace to forgive FDR, and they continued to live together, but their relationship was never again the same. She worked with him to achieve his goals, she was his partner, she was his "lady,"

---

[7] FDR himself used this term to describe his personality. It in no way carried for him the stigma of "sissy."

ER as mother to a growing family

but they slept separately, and she never again let anyone take her for granted.

THE STORY OF LUCY MERCER, AS TOLD BY JOSEPH LASH

Since ER declined to mention Lucy Mercer in her *Autobiography*, even though FDR had been dead many years when she wrote it, we must call upon a close friend of hers to tell the story. Joseph Lash was a young American Socialist during the 1930s. The Student League for Industrial Democracy, with which he was affiliated, worked with American Communists in opposition to the growing Fascist movements in Europe and America until Josef Stalin, Premier of the Soviet Union, made a pact with Germany's Adolf Hitler in 1939. Lash was a puzzled and somewhat disillusioned man when called that year to testify before the House Committee on UnAmerican Affairs. While in Washington he met Eleanor Roosevelt, who took an immediate liking to his open idealism, and for the next two decades was his friend. She told him many intimate details of her life, including perhaps the most important of all for her marriage. It was then when he expressed puzzlement over the First Family's domestic arrangements, how the President and his wife slept apart and in many other ways lived separate lives, she explained to him what happened in 1918. Lash placed the following account in his book *Eleanor and Franklin*. Be prepared for the way Lash, who is a journalist more than a historian, throws a bewildering variety of persons into his account:

> Eleanor employed Lucy Page Mercer, then twenty-two, in the winter season of 1913–1914 to help with social correspondence three mornings a week. Lucy, an efficient social secretary and a charming person, soon became a household familiar. By late spring 1914 Franklin was writing Eleanor in Hyde Park[8] that he had arrived safely in Washington, gone to the house, "and Albert telephoned Miss Mercer who later came and cleaned up." (Albert was the Roosevelt chauffeur and general handyman.)
>
> Sara approved of Lucy. In the spring of 1915 when she came down to stay with the children during Franklin and Eleanor's trip to the San Francisco Exposition, a letter that reported such news as "Babs [Franklin Jr.] is splendid, had his one big movement," also included an enthusiastic reference to Eleanor's social secretary: "Miss Mercer is here, she is *so* sweet and attractive and adores you Eleanor."

✽ ✽ ✽

---

[8] Because Eleanor disliked her role as a Washington Cabinet wife, she lived as much as possible in the Roosevelts' New York home at Hyde Park.

[Lucy] had qualities of femininity that Eleanor lacked, and Eleanor was aware of her own shortcomings. Because she could not relax, others found it difficult to be wholly relaxed with her. Duty came first, not fun or pleasure. She still felt awkward at parties, and at dances she put in an appearance and then vanished. While Arthur Schlesinger, Jr.,[9] may have exaggerated when he described the Eleanor Roosevelt of that era as "a woman sternly devoted to plain living, invincibly 'sensible' in her taste and dress," she herself often spoke of the "Puritan" in her that held her back from high living, frivolity and indolence.

Franklin, on the other hand, was . . . the "gay cavalier," the "lord lover"—debonair, fun-loving, and able to enjoy making a night of it with the British Embassy "boys" or his intimates at the Metropolitan Club. Franklin was one of the handsomest men in Washington, admired by men and women alike. Walter Camp, the famous Yale coach who came to wartime Washington to keep its executives in trim, described Roosevelt as "a beautifully built man, with the long muscles of an athlete." The assistant military attache at the British Embassy, Arthur Murray, spoke of Roosevelt as "breathing health and virility." Bill Phillips remembered him as "always amusing, always the life of the party." After Auntie Bye had seen Franklin in Washington, Admiral Cowles (her husband) reported to Franklin that Bye had thought him brave and charming, "but," Cowles added, "the girls will spoil you soon enough Franklin, and I leave you to them."

Eleanor also teased him about his popularity with the ladies. He was going back to the department at five o'clock, she reported to Sara, to review "the yeomen F" (female).[10] She thought that was entertaining, but she might have been happier had the secretary assumed that duty. When Franklin went to Europe in 1918 she was amused at all the lovely creatures in the Navy Department and the Red Cross who took an interest in his safe arrival abroad. The wife of a Marine captain, she wrote Franklin, "told me she knew you were on the way and had been so worried! She's one of my best cooks on the canteen, so it hasn't interfered with her work!" Everyone was so nice about Franklin's safe arrival in Europe, she reported to Sara: "I wish I could tell you how many people speak as though they were lying awake nights over him!"

---

[9] Schlesinger, a historian, had earlier written an article on the Lucy Mercer affair for *Ladies Home Journal* entitled "FDR's 'Secret Romance.'"

[10] Yeomen are naval petty officers. FDR seemed to enjoy the company of women doing clerical work for the Navy.

She knew that she did not satisfy the frivolous, flirtatious side of Franklin's nature. She liked the company of older people while he complained that they were always invited to the stodgy parties where he was usually given the "honor" of taking the oldest dowager present in to dinner. Her letters from Campobello and Hyde Park[11] were filled with expressions of pleasure that he was having a gay time, which reflected an awareness that companionship and love that were not freely offered were not worth having. But she was also jealous, and undoubtedly the more firmly she urged him to go to a party alone, the more she wanted him to say no. She disciplined herself to treat his flirtations as summer shadows. She had long ago learned to repress her jealousy, to think tolerantly, even fondly, of possible rivals when her adored father had filled his letters from West Virginia with accounts of all the things he did with the little girls in Abingdon. She could treat Franklin's dalliances lightly so long as she was sure of his love, sure that she came first with him.

❋ ❋ ❋

Eleanor was nervous about Lucy Mercer that summer [1917]. When she reluctantly left Washington she put Lucy and Mary Munn in charge of the Saturdays when she gave out yarn and collected the sweaters, scarves, and socks that had been finished. Eleanor had insisted that Lucy, who had begun to work in the Navy Department as a yeoman (F), third class, in June, be paid and that the relationship be strictly a business one. She had given Franklin notes on how she wanted her "wool Saturdays"[12] to be handled while she was away. "Your letter of Thursday is here and one from Miss Mercer," she wrote him on July 23. "Why did you make her waste all that time answering those fool notes? I tore them and the answers up and please tear any other results of my idiocy up at once. She tells me you are going off for Sunday and I hope you all had a pleasant trip but I'm so glad I'm here and not on the Potomac!"

The trip to which Miss Mercer referred combined duty with pleasure. "The trip on the Sylph[13] was a joy and a real rest, though I got in a most satisfactory visit to the fleet," Franklin wrote her.

---

[11] Hyde Park was the Roosevelts' New York home, while Campobello was their island vacation home.
[12] Days for collecting (wool) clothing for the war effort. Eleanor also worked during the war for the Red Cross.
[13] FDR's sailboat.

Such a funny party, but it worked out *wonderfully!* The Charlie Munns, the Cary Graysons, Lucy Mercer and Nigel Law, and they all got on splendidly. We swam about four times and Sunday afternoon went up the James to Richmond. We stopped at Lower and Upper Brandon, Westover and Shirley and went all over them, getting drenched to the skin by several severe thunderstorms. Those old houses are really wonderful but *not* comfy!"

Nigel Law, the third secretary of the British Embassy, was a bachelor and a companion of Franklin's in relaxation at the Chevy Chase Club and at the Lock Tavern Club on the Potomac. Before Eleanor left Washington, she had spent a week end on the *Sylph* at which Lucy Mercer and Nigel Law were present. Did the presence of Nigel Law allay her worry about Lucy?

She was glad he had enjoyed his trip, Eleanor commented, "but sorry you found things not quite right in the fleet. The party sounds delightful to me except the Graysons but I think you were clever to take them." Eleanor's letter went on to talk of household matters such as reminding him to deposit three hundred dollars into the household account on August 1 as she intended to draw on it that day to pay bills, but she did not manage to conceal her disquiet completely. She was writing for train accommodations early, she announced, but he would see very little of her in Washington in the early autumn because she would have lots of things to do in New York. "I think in spite of all their troubles Mrs. Munn and Miss M. like to run my Sats. so I shall have no scruples there and I don't think I shall have to take over the packing room." Then, in a reference to his protestations of how lonely it was in Washington in the summertime, she remarked "I'm glad you are so gay but you know I predicted it! I hope you'll have this Sunday at H.P. [Hyde Park]."

Then Franklin informed her, "I do miss you so very much, but I am getting busier and busier and fear my hoped-for dash to Campo next week for two days will not materialize. Nor can I get to H.P. for Sunday, as I found my absence last Sunday has put me too far back." "I am sorry," she wrote back, "you can't get to H.P. this Sunday before Mama leaves. I know she will feel badly about it. I hope you won't try to come here. It is too far away and you ought not to do it. It will be better to take 2 weeks at H.P. in September and October." But it was a reproach, because only four days earlier she had written, "I am praying no one will come to stay this summer, I am having such a delightful, unbothered time. . . . I wish you could come but I want no one else!" And there was another reproach: "I don't think you read my letters for you never answer a question and nothing I ask for appears!"

Although she was having a "delightful, unbothered time" at Campobello, when Franklin came down with his old throat infection at the end of July, Eleanor rushed to Washington and did not return to Campobello until the middle of August. En route back she wrote, "I hated to leave yesterday. Please go to the doctor twice a week, eat well and sleep well and remember I *count* on seeing you the 26th. My threat was no idle one."

She did not say what her threat had been, but whatever her suspicion of an attachment between her husband and Lucy, it is obvious that she hadn't mentioned it while in Washington, for on August 20 Franklin wrote her, "I had a very occupied Sunday, starting off for golf at 9 with McIlhenny, Legare, and McCawley, quick lunch at Chevy Chase, then in to town and off in car at 2:30 to the Horsey's place near Harper's Ferry. Lucy Mercer went and the Graysons and we got there at 5:30, walked over the farm—a very rich one and run by the two sisters—had supper with them and several neighbors, left at nine and got home at midnight! The day was magnificent, but the road more dusty and even more crowded than when we went to Gettysburg."

This time Franklin did get to Campobello as he had promised. "It is horrid to be without you," Eleanor wrote him on September 2, the day after he left, "and the chicks and I bemoaned our sad fate all through breakfast." But she continued to be reserved and wary toward Lucy, as indicated by a genteel dispute between the two over Eleanor's insistence on paying Lucy for handling her wool Saturdays. Eleanor sent a check, which Lucy declined to accept. Eleanor was immovable and Lucy finally said she would abide by her wishes since Eleanor was mistress of the situation. She apologized for having been unbusinesslike, but then she returned the check as the last two collections were not made, on the assistant secretary's instruction; furthermore, on Saturday, July 21, she had not been present, and she had participated the previous Saturday only to the extent of answering questions and listing what came in. Eleanor sent this letter on to Franklin with the comment, "I've written Miss Mercer and returned the check saying I knew she had done far more work than I could pay for. She is evidently quite cross with me!"

"*You* are entirely disconnected and Lucy Mercer and Mrs. Munn are closing up the loose ends," Franklin replied.

That autumn the Roosevelts moved into a larger house at 2131 R Street, and wool distribution and collection were shifted to rooms at the Navy Department. Lucy Mercer, who had been promoted to yeoman, second class, was released from her Navy duty on October 5, 1917, "by special order of Secretary of the Navy"— perhaps for hardship, since her father had died a few days earlier—but she still helped Eleanor as social secretary and Eleanor still asked her to fill in when she needed an extra woman for a lunch or dinner party.

On the surface all went on as usual, but Eleanor must have had a sense of impending catastrophe. That winter she wrote almost daily to her mother-in-law, whose standards in regard to the obligations that a husband owed his wife and family were precise and unbudgable. Her letters to Sara at this time were as warmly affectionate as they had been the year of her honeymoon. It was as if she were seeking to protect herself against the disaster she saw coming by shielding herself in the older woman's lee.

"Much love always dearest Mummy," Eleanor wrote on January 22, 1918. "I miss you and so do the children, as the years go on I realize how lucky we are to have you and I wish we could always be together. Very few mothers I know mean as much to their daughters as you do to me." "I wish you were always here!" she wrote a month later. "There are always so many things I want to talk over and ask you about and letters are not very satisfactory are they?" She rejoiced when the time came for Sara's spring visit. "We are all thrilled at the thought of having you, I am particularly hungry for a sight of you, only a stern sense of duty has kept me from running away to see you a number of times."

Sara sent Franklin and Eleanor a letter and telegram on their wedding anniversary, and Eleanor replied,

> Thirteen years seems to sound a long time and yet it does not seem long. I often think of what an interesting, happy life Franklin has given me and how much you have done to make our life what it is. As I have grown older I have realized better all you do for us and all you mean to me and the children especially and you will never know how grateful I am nor how much I love you dear.

Sara reciprocated Eleanor's regard.

When Aunt Kassie's daughter, "Little Kassie," married George B. St. George, the latter's mother was delighted with her daughter-in-law. "Well, Kassie, you are running a close second to my Eleanor as a daughter-in-law," Sara commented. Kassie demurred: "Oh, Aunt Sallie, I never could be as good and lovely as Eleanor is."

For some her very goodness was a goad. The romance between Franklin and Lucy did not escape Alice's[14] keen eyes. She saw Franklin out motoring with Lucy, and called him afterward. "I saw you 20 miles out in the country," she teased. "You didn't see me.

---

[14] Alice Roosevelt Longworth, eldest child of President Theodore Roosevelt. She enjoyed a sometimes intense rivalry with her cousin Eleanor.

Your hands were on the wheel but your eyes were on that perfectly lovely lady."

"Isn't she perfectly lovely?" he replied.

Alice encouraged the romance. Franklin dined at Alice's when
Eleanor was out of town, and she also invited Lucy. It was good for
Franklin, Alice maintained. "He deserved a good time. He was married to Eleanor." Moreover, since she considered Eleanor "overly
noble," Alice was not beyond enjoying a little one-upmanship at
Eleanor's expense. Alice and Eleanor had run into each other at
the Capitol, but Eleanor had left Alice at the door, she reported
to Franklin, "not having allowed her to tell me any secrets. She
inquired if you had told me and I said no and that I did not
believe in knowing things which your husband did not wish you
to know so I think I will be spared any further mysterious secrets!"

When Franklin returned from his 1918 trip to Europe in September stricken with double pneumonia, Eleanor took care of his
mail, and in the course of doing so she came upon Lucy's letters.
Her worst fears were confirmed. Her world seemed to break into
pieces. After her wedding there had been a period of total depen-
dency and insecurity from which she had slowly begun to eman-
cipate herself. But Franklin's love was the anchor to which her self-
confidence and self-respect were secured, and now the anchor
was cut. The thought tortured Eleanor that, having borne him six
children, she was now being discarded for a younger, prettier,
gayer woman—that her husband's love belonged to someone
else. The bottom, she wrote, dropped out of her world. She confronted her husband with Lucy's letters. She was prepared to give
her husband his freedom, she told him, if after thinking over what
the consequences might be for the children he still wanted to end
their marriage.

He soon discovered that divorce might have disagreeable consequences in addition to the effect upon the children. Sara was
said to have applied pressure with the threat to cut him off if he
did not give up Lucy. If Franklin was in any doubt about what
a divorce might do to his political career, Howe was there to
enlighten him. Lucy, a devout Catholic, drew back at the prospect
of marriage to a divorced man with five children. Eleanor gave him
a choice—if he did not break off with Lucy, she would insist on a
divorce. Franklin and Lucy agreed never to see each other again.

✳ ✳ ✳

With Eleanor the paramount, perhaps the only, consideration
in preserving the marriage was the children, and no doubt

Franklin's affection for his children was the major reason for his hesitation. Lucy's guilt feelings as a Catholic and Sara's threat were undoubtedly also influential, but for years Eleanor believed that the decisive factor with Franklin had been his realization that a divorce would end his political career.

A long letter dated February 14, 1920, from Eleanor to Sara full of chitchat about the children and political news ended with the sentence, "Did you know Lucy Mercer married Mr. Wintie Rutherfurd two days ago?"

In later years Eleanor confided to her most intimate friends, "I have the memory of an elephant. I can forgive, but I cannot forget."

FDR agreed to give Lucy up, but he never did. He saw her often over the years, visiting with her during holidays away from ER, even having her to dinner at the White House in ER's absence. Lucy's husband, Wintie Rutherfurd, died in 1944; and ER discovered, when FDR died in Georgia in 1945, that Lucy was with him at the end.

She never mentioned the affair to him again. Nor did she ever refer to it publicly. She fulfilled her public role as his wife, but the two never slept together again. When she was asked at the time he died if she loved him, she replied that she had not really loved him since learning of the affair with Lucy.

YEARS OF POLITICAL PREPARATION (1921–1933)

In 1921, three years after the crisis in her marriage, a second event further helped mold Eleanor and Franklin Roosevelt into a couple perfectly matched for the challenges of their life together. While they vacationed on Campobello Island that summer, FDR was stricken with polio, then called infantile paralysis. When it became evident that he would never walk again without aids, ER refused to let him retire to private life in the country, as his mother advised him to do. She encouraged him to continue his political career; and in the months while he made his partial recovery she did his political work for him. She joined the League of Women Voters and the Women's Division of the Democratic Party. She learned the skills that would make her the perfect political complement to him. Frances Perkins, who as FDR's Secretary of Labor from 1933 to 1945 was the first woman to serve in a President's Cabinet, had many opportunities to observe ER's rise to prominence and indispensability to FDR. The following passage from Perkins' memoirs provides a vivid description of the Roosevelt partnership:

> In the years of his illness Mrs. Roosevelt developed a remarkable reportorial quality. She had always been an observant woman. She learned to be more observant and to be able to repeat in detail what she saw and heard. This was of priceless help to him, handicapped as he was, longing to be in touch with the people, and having to learn to take vicarious instead of direct personal experience. The friends who became most useful to him were those who reported truthfully, colorfully, on what they saw and heard. His own sympathy and imagination built on these reports. Mrs. Roosevelt realized that in his invalid period he needed all the help and strengthening that could come to him through his mind. With great perspicacity she brought him people with whom he could share the things going on in his mind. She realized she could introduce new and stimulating ideas through people who were thoughtful, had had a variety of experience, and wanted to know what he thought.
>
> ✳ ✳ ✳
>
> During this time Mrs. Roosevelt broadened her own social and political contacts—she made a habit of keeping in touch with party activities in the state. She entered into local campaign work. She made a broad political acquaintance; she was anxious to keep her husband's interest in political affairs alive. It had been his primary concern, and she saw in it something he could build on as he began to recover. She was well aware that if one is ill and out of things too long one is forgotten, and she made, I think, a determined effort to keep alive Franklin Roosevelt's name and good reputation within the party.

Eleanor Roosevelt's Own Account

In the following passage from her *Autobiography*, ER herself describes those years of the 1920s when she learned politics, kept her husband's name alive in political circles, and trained herself for future responsibilities. As always when speaking of herself, she describes events in a matter-of-fact, chatty tone, as if she were describing the life of an ordinary person, not the famous person she became.

Dr. Draper [the doctor who first treated FDR's paralysis] felt strongly that it was better for Franklin to make the effort to take an active part in life again and lead, as far as possible, a normal life, with the interests that had always been his. Even if it tired him, it was better for his general condition.

The previous January Franklin had accepted an offer made by Mr. Van Lear Black to become vice-president of the Fidelity and Deposit Company of Baltimore, in charge of the New York office, and he had worked there until his illness. Mr. Black was a warm friend and kept his place for him until he was well enough to resume his work.

Mr. Howe[15] felt that the one way to get my husband's interest aroused was to keep him as much as possible in contact with politics. This seemed to me an almost hopeless task. However, in order to accomplish his ends Mr. Howe began to urge me to do some political work again. I could think of nothing I could do but during the spring I was thrown on two or three occasions with a young woman who interested me considerably. Her name was Marion Dickerman. She was interested in working conditions for women and she taught in a school. I, too, was interested in working conditions for women, harking back to the interests of my girlhood. Mrs. James Lees Laidlaw asked me to attend a luncheon of the Women's Trade Union League and become an associate member. I joined the organization and have been a member ever since. This luncheon was my second contact with some of the women whom I had first met in Washington at the International Conference for Working Women and this resulted in a long association. I have never lost touch with this group. Many of them were interested in politics, and I soon found that Marion Dickerman also was interested.

Through my acquaintance with Miss Dickerman I met her friend Nancy Cook. Miss Cook invited me to preside at a luncheon to raise funds for the women's division of the Democratic State Committee. I had been carrying on to a limited extent my work for the League of Women Voters, but I had never done anything for a political organization before nor had I ever made a speech in any sizable gathering. Here I found myself presiding at a luncheon, without the faintest idea of what I was going to say or what work the organization was really doing. That was the beginning of a warm and lasting friendship with both Miss Dickerman

---

[15] Louis Howe, aide and adviser both to Eleanor and to Franklin, will be discussed fully in later accounts.

and Miss Cook, and through them I met Miss Harriet May Mills and Mrs. Caroline O'Day and went to work with the Democratic women of New York State.

* * *

Through my interest in the League of Women Voters, the Trade Union League and the Democratic State Committee, where now I had become finance chairman, I was beginning to find the political contacts that Louis [Howe] wanted. I drove a car on election day and brought people to the polls. I began to learn a good deal about party politics in a small place. It was rather sordid in spots. I worked with our county committee and our associate county chairwoman. I saw how people took money or its equivalent on election day for their votes and how much of the party machinery was geared to crooked business. On the other hand, I saw hard work and unselfish public service and fine people in unexpected places. I learned again that human beings are seldom all good or all bad and that few human beings are incapable of rising to the heights now and then.

* * *

During those years before Franklin went back actively into politics a number of things I did were undertaken at Louis Howe's suggestion in order to interest Franklin. The organization of state campaigns was primarily my job and, again with Louis Howe's help, I thought up some of the best stunts that were undertaken. For instance, in the campaign of 1924 [for governor of New York] Alfred E. Smith was running against my cousin, Theodore Roosevelt, Jr., who had previously been Assistant Secretary of the Navy in the Harding administration. The recent Teapot Dome[16] scandal—with which Theodore Roosevelt, Jr., had nothing to do—had created much excitement; so, capitalizing on this, we had a framework resembling a teapot, which spouted steam, built on top of an automobile and it led the procession of cars which toured the state, following the Republican candidate for governor wherever he went!

In the thick of political fights one always feels that all methods of campaigning that are honest are fair, but I do think this was a rough stunt and I never blamed my cousin when he retaliated in later campaigns against my husband.

---

[16] Republican Secretary of the Interior Albert Fall was in 1922 caught profiting from illegal sale of U.S. oil reserves at a facility called Teapot Dome in Wyoming.

It was during these years, too, that I became engaged in two enterprises with Nancy Cook and Marion Dickerman. Franklin was particularly interested in one of our undertakings. He helped to design and build a stone cottage beside a brook where we often went to picnic during the first years after he was paralyzed. The brook was called Val-Kill, so we called the cottage Val-Kill Cottage. Franklin was the contractor and the builder and, though Mr. Henry Toombs was the architect, he liked to talk over every detail. We built not only the cottage but a swimming pool in which the children and occasionally Franklin enjoyed much sport. Later we built a more elaborate pool, but by that time Franklin was the President and we had to conform to the regulations set up by his doctor and put in filtration machinery. I do not think we had any more fun, however, in the bigger and more elaborate pool than we had in the original small one, the building of which my husband had supervised.

The cottage was not an end in itself. It was the place in which Nancy Cook and Marion Dickerman lived and from which Miss Cook directed a furniture factory. Nancy Cook was an attractive woman who could do almost anything with her hands. She had long wanted to make reproductions of Early American furniture. We obtained help and co-operation from the Metropolitan Museum, the Hartford Museum, and from many individuals. We produced drawings and went to look at famous pieces of old furniture. Miss Cook had no desire to reproduce worm-eaten antiques; she wanted to use methods employed by our ancestors, and see whether she could find a market for furniture which, though the first processes were done by machinery would be largely handmade and therefore expensive. Because the finishing was all done by hand, the wood looked and felt as though it bad been used and polished for years.

My husband was greatly interested in finding some industry that could be developed in country areas such as ours, and that could perhaps furnish occupation for some of the younger men who would otherwise leave the farms. By giving them work in an industry which would yield them a fairly good income during the slack period on the farms, he thought one could keep the progressive, more active group of young people working steadily and so raise the standard of farm development in our area.

He had a great love for the soil and wanted to see it developed; but he realized that many of the farmers around us had a difficult time holding their young sons on the land, because the return for hard and strenuous work was meager. His interest in our enterprise was therefore in the training and the employment of young men in the vicinity.

Nancy Cook ran the enterprise and I put in most of the capital from my earnings from radio and writing and even used some of the small capital that I had inherited from my mother and father. The others, especially Nancy Cook, contributed what they could afford.

We kept the factory going all through the early depression years, when the employment of people seemed vitally important. At last Miss Cook found that carrying two jobs—she was also executive secretary of the women's division of the Democratic State Committee—was too much for her, so we closed the shop.

My husband's object was not achieved, and I think the idea has been proved impractical on a much larger scale in some of the homesteads which were started during the depression. Some succeeded but few returned on the original investment. Nevertheless, in the crisis they took people off relief and gave them back self-respect and a sense of security—a considerable achievement.

Although this experiment was a disappointment to Franklin, he accepted the failure philosophically both in our own case and later in the case of the country-wide experiment. I think he felt regret; but, with the same acceptance of the inevitable which he showed in so many other matters, having tried the experiment and become satisfied that it did not work, he gave it up and sought other solutions. He hoped that some day it might work out. He always accepted things as they were and set such experiences aside as something to remember and perhaps use in the future.

I never made any money out of this furniture-making venture. In fact, I was probably one of the best customers the shop had, because I bought various pieces of furniture as wedding presents and as gifts for other occasions.

During the depression I took over the factory building and was able, through my earnings, to turn it into a fairly comfortable if somewhat odd house. Though I did not have any architectural advice, I did have the help of a friend, Henry Osthagen, an engineer. We used local labor entirely. Employing people seemed the best way to spend some of the money I was able to earn during those years. Part of the shop we made into an apartment for my secretary, Malvina Thompson, and I frequently went there to work quietly with her; the rest of the building became a guest cottage, which we used when the big house was overcrowded—something that often happened during the years when my husband was President. Since turning the old Hyde Park house over to the government, I have made the converted shop building my year-round home.

During the early years of my acquaintance with Nancy Cook and Marion Dickerman I became associated in the Todhunter School with Miss Dickerman, who was first the assistant principal and then the principal. It was a private school for girls from the primary grades through high school. Miss Todhunter, who was British, finally sold the school to Marion Dickerman, Nancy Cook and myself and went back to England. I began teaching there in 1927. I taught only the older girls because I considered that it took far less training to teach them than to teach the younger children. I gave courses in American history and in English and American literature and later we tried some courses in current events which I hope were more practical than are many of the courses given to sixteen- and seventeen-year-old girls. We visited the New York City courts and I think many young people learned a great deal from sitting in one of the children's courts for an hour. Those whom their parents allowed to go I took to see the various kinds of tenements that exist in a city like New York, as well as the big markets and various other places. All this made the government of the city something real and alive, rather than just words in a textbook.

Lorena Hickock's Account

ER's account of these years of preparation for public life sound quite commonplace. They are devoid of any deep analysis of cause and effect. Fortunately, we have other accounts, from close confidants, of this period. Her return to public service after the years of serving primarily as a wife and mother, the transformation from private person to public figure, during the decade of the 1920s, is told with great clarity by ER's friend, the journalist Lorena Hickock, whom ER affectionately called Hick. The relationship of ER to Hickock has long been a subject of speculation. Hickock became ER's close friend in 1932, when the Associated Press assigned her to cover ER as the Roosevelts were about to enter the White House. After a time she decided to end her journalistic work and become ER's assistant because she felt she could no longer be objective about a woman she loved so dearly. Their letters tell the story. ER to Hick: "Tonight you sounded so far away and formal. Oh! I want to put my arms around you. I ache to hold you close. Your ring is a great comfort. I look at it and think she does love me, or I wouldn't be wearing it!" Hick to ER: "I've been trying today to bring back your face—to remember just how you looked. . . . Most clearly I remember your eyes, with the kind of teasing smile in them, and the feeling of that soft spot just northeast of the corner of your mouth against my lips." And ER to Hick: "Dearest, strong relationships have to grow strong deep roots. We are growing them now, partly because we are separated. The foliage and the flowers will come somehow, I'm sure of it."

But at some spot, perhaps before a physical relationship developed, ER pulled back from Hickock. She feared for the rest of her life that she had led her on, and that caused her great pain. The intimacy ceased, yet they continued to be friends, and together they wrote the book *Ladies of Courage,* published in 1954. It featured chapters about the leading women of American history: Elizabeth Cady Stanton, Susan B. Anthony, Helen Gahagan Douglas, Molly Dewson,[17] and Eleanor Roosevelt. Hickock alone wrote the chapter "A Political Profile of Mrs. Eleanor Roosevelt," but her information came from her years of contact with her subject. Hickock was no objective historian. Her account of ER's preparation for public life is always appreciative and admiring. But she does write clearly, perceptively, and analytically. She completes the picture of ER in training for her later roles in life:

> During the years while her young husband was in the New York State Senate and while he was Assistant Secretary of the Navy, her interest in politics was probably about what it would have been in any business or profession in which he was engaged. It never occurred to her that she had any part to play beyond keeping the household running smoothly, entertaining his political friends, and being a good listener. Since he was for woman suffrage, she supposed she was, too, although she privately doubted that women would ever amount to much in politics.

* * *

> Her husband's illness in 1921 brought Louis Howe[18] into their household. The two men had become friends while Roosevelt was in the state senate and Howe was an Albany newspaper correspondent. Howe was greatly impressed with a fight the youthful sena-

---

[17] ER first met Mary (Molly) Dewson in 1924, when she was civic secretary to the Women's City Club of New York. She later played a large role in FDR's New Deal.
[18] Howe remained an assistant to both Franklin and Eleanor until his death in 1936. He even lived in the White House from 1933 to 1936.

tor from Duchess County had led against the forces of Tammany Hall in the legislature and is said to have pointed him out to Mrs. Howe in church one Sunday with the remark, "There's a young man with a future." He began then his inconspicuous and extremely important contribution to that future, working always behind the scene as political adviser and friend. Mrs. Roosevelt could not understand what her husband saw in the frail, stooped little man with the asthmatic cough and irascible bark. His untidiness annoyed her—he smoked incessantly and dropped cigarette ashes on his vest. Howe accompanied them to Washington, took a job in the Navy Department, and remained behind after the Harding victory to wind up administrative details. He was about to go back into the newspaper business when Roosevelt was stricken with infantile paralysis while vacationing on Campobello Island in New Brunswick. He went immediately to Campobello, made arrangements for the patient's transfer to New York with the least possible publicity, dropped his own plans, and announced that he was standing by. Unable to find a suitable New York apartment that he could afford, he settled his family in Poughkeepsie and moved in with the Roosevelts, to remain until his death in 1936.

Almost immediately a tug-of-war developed between the sick man's mother and his friend. She was convinced that her son's political career was over and determined that he retire to Hyde Park and let her take care of him. Howe was just as determined that he should not. He had little difficulty convincing Mrs. Eleanor Roosevelt that her husband might lapse into permanent invalidism if he settled down at Hyde Park. He was going to have to make a difficult adjustment, and it was important that he be kept in touch with the things in which he had always been interested. He needed politics and people, and since for the time being he could not go to them, they would have to be brought to him. "And that," Howe told her, "is something you will have to do."

Appalled as she was at the idea of getting out and mixing in politics, Mrs. Roosevelt was probably better prepared for it mentally than she realized. For, after they moved back to New York the winter before her husband's illness, she had found herself so bored with formal society and the genteel charities her mother-in-law considered suitable for her that she had begun to grope for some new outlet for her energy. She started taking cooking lessons and a course in stenography. Mrs. Frank Vanderlip, state chairman of the recently organized League of Women Voters, invited her to become a member of the board and, since she had been living in Washington for eight years, suggested that she prepare a monthly report on national legislation. To her embarrassed confession that she knew nothing about national legislation, Mrs. Vanderlip replied that she would have the help of a very able woman lawyer, Miss Elizabeth Read, who would go through the *Congressional Record* and mark the bills in which the League was interested, send for copies of them, and explain them to her if necessary. A few days later Mrs. Roosevelt walked shyly into Miss Read's office. For the rest of the winter she spent one morning a week there, poring over the material laid out for her, taking home for further study the bills she did not fully understand. Miss Read was both helpful and encouraging, and they quickly became friends.

* * *

Her first opportunity to go into politics came not long after Louis Howe had convinced her that it was her duty. She was asked to preside at a money-raising luncheon for the Women's Division of the Democratic State Committee. The women thought they could be more effective if they were self-supporting and could plan and carry on their work with less masculine domination. They needed for their luncheon a chairman with social contacts who might bring in substantial contributions. An indication of Mrs. Roosevelt's political obscurity at the time may be taken from the fact that, as they were casting about for a chairman, someone asked if Franklin Roosevelt had a wife! It must have taken every ounce of courage she could muster, for she had never faced an audience before, but she presided at their luncheon, which brought in $12,000.

From that day until she moved to Washington, she was responsible for raising the Women's Division budget, and the New York Democratic women were in the enviable position of having their own money, to spend as they saw fit. She was too inexperienced when she took it on to realize that getting money out of women to support a women's organization is one of the toughest jobs in politics. To her it was a job that needed to be done, and she went ahead and did it to the best of her ability. The amount she was able to raise was not great, and it had to be supplemented by the men during campaigns, but it did give the women more influence and self-respect.

They gave her a desk at headquarters, and inevitably the jobs that found their way to that desk were not confined to money-raising. In characteristic fashion, she took each one on as it came along. She very quickly learned not to leave too much water in the sponge and to pass it lightly over a strip of stamps or the flaps of envelopes to be sealed, and her folding and stuffing had a professional speed and competence. She set aside a definite period in each week for work at headquarters and always showed up when she said she would. Never was there a more dependable volunteer.

One of the by-products of politics, new and absorbing friendships, she found infinitely satisfying. She was as busy as a woman could be, for her husband's illness had greatly increased her family responsibilities, about which she was exceedingly conscientious. But by planning each day down to the last minute, she was able to continue and expand her political activities. She was as diffident in her attitude toward the women she was now meeting as she had been in the beginning with Miss Read and Miss Lape. For many of them were business or professional women, and for any woman who could earn her own living had a respect as profound as her dissatisfaction with what she regarded as her own inadequacies. "If I had to go out and earn my own living, I doubt if I'd even make a very good cleaning woman," she once said bitterly. "I have no talents, no experience, no training for anything."

* * *

Louis Howe had undertaken her political education and was doing a thorough and painstaking job of it. He even taught her how to read a newspaper. "Unless the story deals with a subject in which you are really interested, you don't have to read beyond the first paragraph," he told her—no doubt because she protested that she didn't have time to read the papers, as he insisted she should. He then explained to her the classic structure of a newspaper story, with the "who-what-when-where-how" in the lead. As a result, Mrs. Roosevelt can go through the New York *Times* in the half hour or less she allots for breakfast and give you the gist of its contents. Louis Howe taught her how to write persuasive letters, how to boil down an issue into a brief, clear statement the average person could understand. Making speeches was her most serious difficulty. Since she disliked being conspicuous as much as Howe himself did, she would probably have abandoned the effort had he not kept after her. So she went miserably along with it, the palms of her hands clammy with perspiration every time she had to stand up on a platform. When she was relaxed she had a decidedly pleasing voice, but when she was tense, as she always was before an audience, it would become high and shrill, with a nervous little laugh. Howe would go along, sit in the back row, and lecture her afterward. "Keep your voice down," he would say, "and for Heaven's sake stop that silly giggling." While she was in the White House she finally learned to place her voice properly by working with a coach and she lost the giggle in the process of becoming one of the country's more experienced speakers.

His advice on the contents of a speech was brief and simple— "Say what you have to say and sit down." She learned to speak without a written text and has rarely used one in all the speaking she has done. In 1941, when she was to speak for the Women's Division of the Democratic National Committee at a regional conference in St. Paul, she reluctantly agreed to write her speech in advance. Since the meeting was held in an area where there was widespread hostility to the draft and our other defense preparations and to our aid to Britain, the women knew that the newspapers would want copies of her speech. It arrived ahead of her and was as wooden and uninspiring as she had predicted it would be. "How is the speech?" she asked as she climbed into a taxi at the airport. "I know," she said in the embarrassed silence. After lunch she shut herself up in her hotel room for the afternoon. She carried a few little pieces of paper in her hand as she walked out onto the platform in the St. Paul Armory. For more than an hour a huge audience, in which the America First[19] leaders had planted hecklers after picketing the Armory, listened quietly and attentively to what she had to say.

Mrs. Roosevelt gives Louis Howe all the credit for whatever contribution she may have made to politics—a contribution which she would say is small and unimportant, considering the effort he put into her training. But anyone who has watched her through the years would insist that she has an innate instinct for politics as natural to her as breathing. It had to be brought out and cultivated, and this he was able to do. But it must have been there even in her awkward, unhappy girlhood and during her years as a young wife, completely lacking in self-confidence and preoccupied with her home and family. Dormant as it was, it may have been visible to some discerning eyes, for many years ago her aunt, Corinne Roosevelt Robinson, said to the writer: "Eleanor was always my brother Ted's favorite niece. She is more like him than any of his own children." Nor could it have escaped Louis Howe, for otherwise he would hardly have had the patience to bother with her once his goal had been achieved: getting her husband, whose career he had made his own life work, through a difficult adjustment.

---

[19] America First opposed U.S. involvement in World War II, advocating continued isolationism.

* * *

By 1928 her training and progress as a practicing politician had carried her to the point where Belle Moscowitz[20] asked her to take charge of the women's organization work at national headquarters during the Smith campaign. The job was completely to her liking, although it involved endless hours of what most women would have regarded as slavery at her desk in the General Motors building. She seldom had to appear in public and was not expected to make speeches, except to fill in at the last moment when some other woman dropped out. She made one trip to St. Louis with the Smiths. John J. Raskob, chairman of the National Committee, had observed that very little work was being done among the women in the Middle West, and had persuaded her friend Molly Dewson to go out and take charge. Working happily and inconspicuously behind the scenes, she was finally dragged out into the lime-light when Smith decided it would improve his chances to carry New York State if her husband ran for governor. By this time Franklin Roosevelt had begun to make almost incredible progress in his fight to regain the use of his legs, and there appeared to be a possibility of still great improvement if he continued his treatment at Warm Springs. He was at Warm Springs when the Democrats met in Rochester to nominate a candidate for governor.

Frances Perkins, who earlier described for us the nature of FDR and ER's public partnership, recalled in her memoirs that first race for governor, when all Democrats were supposed to lose but FDR squeaked out a victory, in part because of ER:

She was a great help to her husband in his first gubernatorial campaign. She had already developed the ability to go about among people in a natural, simple, cordial way. When they visited the State Fair, Roosevelt, the nominee, would drive around the grounds to shake hands with many people, while Mrs. Roosevelt would go through the buildings where the livestock, the patchwork quilts, the canned vegetables and preserves, the prize ears of corn were shown. She would ask questions about schools and health and recreation facilities. Her unaffected approach to people won friends at every level.

---

[20] Moscowitz was a public relations operative in the office of New York Governor and 1928 Democratic presidential nominee Al Smith.

Lorena Hickock takes up the story once more and describes the four years as First Lady of New York in Albany:

When her husband became governor, Mrs. Roosevelt took on a routine that would have been fantastic for a woman less disciplined and without her remarkable physical endurance. She could not bear to give up her teaching job, for it meant that she now had a profession, and would not have exchanged for anything in the world the feeling of self-respect it gave her. So when school was in session she would take a Sunday evening train from Albany or Poughkeepsie, arrive in New York around midnight, spend three days at the Todhunter School, and return to Albany Wednesday evening to take up her duties as hostess at the Executive Mansion. How she managed to do it only Mrs. Roosevelt would know, but she also continued to raise the Democratic Women's Division budget and help out at headquarters when she was needed, although she stayed strictly in the background when her husband ran for re-election in 1930. The Women's Division started a small monthly magazine, and Louis Howe taught her how to paste up the dummy for the printers. Years later in the White House she would hurry up from dinner in a long, trailing evening gown, lay out the proofs, shears, paste and ruler on the coffee table in her sitting room and go to work on that dummy, while Louis Howe sat nearby writing the captions—something, she says, he never quite trusted her to do.

Her own education entered a new and more important field during the Albany years, and this time her husband was her teacher. Never was there a public official who had a greater urge to go and see things for himself than Franklin Roosevelt had—an urge that led him to take dangerous and exhausting trips during World II that no other man with his physical handicap would have dreamed of undertaking. Every summer while he was governor of New York he would take a motor trip around the state, inspecting everything from hospitals and prisons to highway construction jobs. He took Mrs. Roosevelt along, and, arriving at an institution, he would invite the superintendent into his car for a drive around the grounds and send her inside to look things over. His appetite for details was insatiable. "Did you look into the pots and see if they were getting it?" he would demand after he had asked her what the inmates were being fed and she had told him what was on the menu. No trained inspector ever gave an institution a more professional going over than she learned to do, as she stalked about, raising the lids to peer inside the kettles on the stove, turning back beds to finger blankets and linen and see if they were clean, looking into corners and cupboards, opening closet doors, taking stock of exits and fire escapes. She learned to watch people, too, to study postures and facial expressions, to find out what was going on inside a person's mind with a few seemingly innocuous questions. By the time they went to Washington, Franklin Roosevelt had in his wife a reliable, intelligent and superbly trained reporter, equipped to do the most important job he would ever ask her to undertake.

An Assessment of the Early Years, by Tamara Hareven

Because of her training throughout the 1920s including her four years as First Lady of New York, Eleanor Roosevelt was perhaps the best-prepared First Lady in American history. She was also the most reform-minded of First Ladies, having developed a social conscience before World War I and having defined her approaches to reform during the 1920s. Her path, her preparation to be a reformer, is best reconstructed by Clark University Professor of History Tamara Hareven, who has written a biography entitled *Eleanor Roosevelt: An American Conscience*. The following excerpt is from Dr. Hareven's essay "ER and Reform" in the book *Without Precedent: The Life and Career of Eleanor Roosevelt*. Dr. Hareven's thesis is that ER's greatest contribution to American history was her commitment to reform:

Preoccupied with her family, in the period before World War I she considered politics a "sinister affair," about which she professed to know so little that she could not explain to inquiring Europeans the relationship between the federal government and the states. In her autobiography she never mentioned the intellectual background of the age, nor referred to books of the period that might have influenced her. When describing [her uncle] Theodore Roosevelt's greatness as a leader in a history book she began writing in 1929, she ignored his role as a Progressive reformer.

During World War I, her work for the Red Cross jolted her dormant social conscience.[21] Her real apprenticeship to reform

---

[21] Dormant since her work at the Rivington Settlement House, which ended with her marriage in 1905.

occurred later, though, during the 1920s, following her husband's crippling illness, when efforts to maintain Franklin Roosevelt's contact with politics involved her in reform work and political training. By this time she had demonstrated a sensitivity to human suffering, an indignation over poverty, and a readiness to serve. But she still lacked intellectual commitment and mainstream political experience.

Her training during this decade began with the Women's City Club of New York and League of Women Voters, whose members taught her how to compile and analyze legislation. Through work with Louis Howe, the New York Women's Democratic Committee, and the New York State and National Democratic Committees (especially through her campaign work for Al Smith) she learned the political realities and the mechanisms by which reform could be achieved. In her work with the New York settlement houses, she developed close ties with Lillian Wald, founder of the Henry Street Settlement, and Mary Simkhovitch, head worker at the Greenwich House. The settlement work focused her attention on the complexity of urban problems and on the interrelationships among poor housing, poverty, crime, and disease. Through their example of personal devotion and service, the settlement workers convinced her that for future reform a sense of personal responsibility to one's community and social service was as important as legislation. Surprisingly, the settlement workers did not inspire in her a lasting interest in immigrants, toward whom they were directing most of their efforts.

From the National Consumers' League,[22] Eleanor Roosevelt learned the value of social investigation and exposé as first steps toward reform. Her guide, the league's founder and president, Florence Kelley, took Roosevelt on visits to politicians and legislatures in the campaign to protect women in industry and to abolish child labor. She instilled in Roosevelt her faith in the power of the boldly stated fact and insisted that information was half the way to reform. The conception of the reformer as investigator and educator, inspired by Florence Kelley, emerged as a central feature of Eleanor Roosevelt's reform work. Through Rose Schneiderman, president of the New York branch of the Women's Trade Union League (WTUL), Roosevelt became familiar with the trade unions, formed her commitment to the rights of labor, and adopted the

---

[22] An organization committed to serving the needs of U.S. citizens by publishing information about the safety, effectiveness, and pricing of consumer products.

definition of a "living wage" that included—in addition to food, housing, and clothing—considerations such as education, recreation, and emergency needs, especially for sickness and accidents. This was the beginning of her lifelong support of the WTUL and of fair labor standards. The 1920s exposed her to idealist reformers—both survivors of the Progressive Era and a new generation of professional social workers and political activists.

Eleanor Roosevelt's apprenticeship in the 1920s was crucial for her own development as a reformer, and for the access that reformers and reform movements gained to the New Deal programs. Later, through her own experience and her presence, she would provide a channel through which the energies of the voluntary reform associations and their leaders could move into the New Deal's reform program and machinery. As a result of her own training and through her own career, Eleanor Roosevelt thus provided an important bridge between earlier Progressive ideals, the reform movements of the 1920s, and the New Deal.

Eleanor Roosevelt plunged into social reform without a clearly formulated philosophy, a plan, or a program. Driven by idealism, she embarked on social reform and political activities at a point in her life when, like some other women reformers, she was experiencing a void in her life—a need to be active beyond the domestic sphere. In her case, the plunge into reform was also an escape from the pain of discovering her husband's affair with Lucy Mercer in 1918. She was also pushed into reform and political activity by the architects of her husband's political career following his polio attack. Thus, the timing of her entry into the reform scene at the point in her personal life at which she entered, and the historic moment in American reform at which she entered, were crucial for the subsequent course of her career as a reformer.

Underlying Roosevelt's social concern was her humanitarianism, her identification with the suffering of individuals, and a commitment to social justice. She transcended the view of her class and of her generation that poverty was a manifestation of personal failure. From Progressive reformers she adopted the view that poverty was a social problem, a result of inequality and of the maldistribution of economic resources. ER had already developed these convictions at an earlier point, but the shock of the Great Depression in itself had an important transforming effect on her social ideas. It marked her transition from sporadic activity in civic affairs and politics to a commitment to social reform. She had seen misery and poverty before, but had assumed that the system was sound, that slums, crime, poverty, and labor problems were blotches that could be removed through the dedication of social workers and legislation. The depression forced her to the soul-shattering realization that something was wrong in the system itself: she began to question the very assumptions of American society and culture.

QUESTIONS FOR RESPONSIVE ESSAYS

1. How did her early life, its advantages and its tragedies, help mold the person we know as the historical Eleanor Roosevelt? How might she have responded differently to the advantages and reacted differently to the tragedies?

2. What things were expected of an early twentieth-century aristocratic American woman? How did and how did not ER fulfill those expectations? How did her responses to the expectations form the public woman she became?

3. How did ER react to the life she faced as FDR's wife and Sara Delano Roosevelt's daughter-in-law? How did she finally come to terms with it? How did it contribute, positively and negatively, to her later public life?

4. How did the Lucy Mercer affair affect ER's life and her relationship with FDR? To what degree, given our knowledge of their personalities, does it seem an inevitable crisis? How did it help create the "team" ER and FDR would form for the rest of their lives? How did ER use her early social activism as a guide for the new life she faced?

5. What was ER's reaction to FDR's polio and the new life he had to lead? Why and how did she train herself for a new life as well? What attitudes did she bring to her renewed activism from her years in social work? What was her role in the Roosevelt "team" that won the governorship of New York and the presidency of the United States?

PART II

First Lady of the United States (1933–1945)

If you prepare yourself at every point as well as you can, with whatever means you may have, however meager they may seem, you will be able to grasp opportunity for broader experience when it appears.

—ELEANOR ROOSEVELT
Autobiography, 1961

Her presence during the Roosevelt years was everywhere. But her real influence was spiritual, not one of laws, appointments, the management of great government bureaus. She was like a warming gulf stream.

—JOSEPH LASH
Without Precedent, 1984

ELEANOR ROOSEVELT AND OTHER FIRST LADIES

From the beginning of the American republic until 1933, when Eleanor Roosevelt came to the White House, the wives of Presidents played a well-defined role in the nation's social and cultural life. Martha Custis Washington set the pattern for First Ladies when she played the part, as she knew the late eighteenth century expected her to do, of "official wife" to the first chief executive. She was not a truly public figure, except in her husband's reflected glory, and she never made her opinions known publicly.

Second First Lady Abigail Adams, who in her letters can be seen to be a woman of strong opinions, for the most part limited her words to the privacy of her bedroom and husband's ear. Dolley Madison, wife of the fourth President and the first wife to live in the White House, established the tradition that the First Lady is the official presidential hostess. After the passing of the loquacious and gregarious Dolley, it was impossible for another President to live in the White House without a First Lady to entertain for him, as had the third President, widower Thomas Jefferson, even if a President had to name a daughter, daughter-in-law, or sister to fill the role.

Although every President except Jefferson has had a First Lady, only a few are remembered by the general reading public today. Only professional historians know much about the majority of First Ladies between Dolley Madison (1809–1817) and Mary Todd Lincoln (1861–1865). Mrs. Lincoln is remembered in part because she occupied the White House during the Civil War, the time of the nation's greatest trauma, and in part because she was the first First Lady to lose her husband to assassination. She also is remembered for her fear that she would be considered a rude frontier woman by "eastern snobs" and therefore spent lavishly to make sure that White House furnishings and her own wardrobe left no doubt of her sophistication. In her last years many of her contemporaries considered her mentally unstable, and she left behind a rather sad image that historians still debate.

The general reading public dwells little on First Ladies from Mrs. Lincoln to Edith Galt Wilson (1916–1921), President Woodrow Wilson's second First Lady. The second Mrs. Wilson, also a First Lady during an important war, is discussed widely because just after World War I her husband suffered a stroke and for a year was unable to tend to his duties. During that time Mrs. Wilson carried messages to and from the President's sickbed, leading to much speculation as to whether she may have been acting in his behalf. She denied during the many years she lived following Wilson's death that she had ever been more than his wife and messenger, a traditional First Lady. Still some contemporaries wondered, as do historians today.

The role of First Lady began to grow as the twentieth century unfolded, as the United States grew internally and in world influence, as the office of President grew in power and prestige. Still most First Ladies, through Mrs. Herbert Hoover (1929–1933), continued to play the traditional public role of devoted domestic companion to the President. They may have espoused the occasional charity, but they did not champion causes, certainly not controversial ones. Then in March 1933, in the middle of the greatest economic depression America has known, Franklin Roosevelt was inaugurated President—and his wife, Eleanor, became First Lady. Although she said, "I never wanted to be a president's wife," she appeared as buoyant and ready to serve as he. She was a new kind of First Lady. While she served in the traditional role of White House hostess, while she was always "ladylike" in manner, appearance, and speech, she had a mind of her own and did not hesitate to speak it, both privately to FDR and in the public arena.

She held her own news conferences; she wrote articles and columns for magazines and newspapers; and she led social causes, many of them politically controversial. She visited people in need, she supported the rights of women and minorities, and she pushed her husband to be proactive even when his New Deal advisers cautioned against it. She served as her husband's eyes and ears; and for twelve years she was chief liaison between the public and the government. And she made her new role popular. Despite the virulence of her critics, every poll taken between 1933 and 1945, and many taken afterward, found her the most admired woman in America—and among the most admired of all public figures. In 1939 it was found that two-thirds of all Americans approved her role as First Lady, a higher percentage than approved FDR's role as President.

An Account of How Eleanor Roosevelt Changed the Role of First Lady, by Abigail McCarthy

Almost from the day Eleanor Roosevelt left the White House in 1945, certainly in the years since her death in 1962, scholars have tried to assess the whys and hows of her revolutionary term as First Lady. Among the more perceptive of these evaluations is the following by Abigail McCarthy. McCarthy is a columnist for the magazine *Commonweal;* and she wrote this essay for the book *Without Precedent: The Life and Career of Eleanor Roosevelt.*

Eleanor Roosevelt was First Lady for over twelve years—longer than any other woman—and during a period crucial in our history. She was at the heart of change, and often its source. No other First Lady has had her influence. No other has been so much the center of controversy. No other has so affected the lives of the women who followed her.

There is general agreement that Eleanor Roosevelt had a pivotal influence on the role of the First Lady: we measure not only her successors but her predecessors by her character and achievements. In 1976 I talked about this with the wives of the twelve candidates for the presidency—women who ranged in politics from Joan Mondale to Nancy Reagan and in background from Eunice Shriver to LaDonna Harris. I spoke with Ella Udall and Cornelia Wallace; Helen Jackson and Bethine Church; Rosalynn Carter and Marvella Bayh; the then First Lady, Betty Ford, and Beryl Bentsen. I also talked with former First Lady Lady Bird Johnson and former vice-presidential wives Muriel Humphrey and Barbara Bush. Inevitably, when talk turned to their conception of the First Lady's role, they mentioned the deep influence of Eleanor Roosevelt: "Of course, since Eleanor Roosevelt. . . . " It was a recurring phrase.

Today, we take certain aspects of the First Lady's role for granted. Although she is not elected or appointed, the First Lady has all the obligations of office and directs not only a household staff but an office staff provided for in the budget of the United States. From the day of her husband's election until the day she dies, she is accompanied by security agents. Her travel is carefully planned. During his tenure of office her every move is scrutinized by the press. She represents the nation both at home and abroad. Her tastes, her preferences, her sense of place in history affect ours.

Being First Lady is not a casual or part-time occupation, but a full-time job. The elevation to this high status comes quickly and, obviously, without any real preparation. Betty Ford spoke of this from her own experience. Just at that time in life when "most mothers of families can look forward to a little time for themselves," she noted, "all of a sudden, I have a full-time job—a job I didn't choose or plan for." Her life, she said, was like a corporate executive's: "I'm at my desk every day, and busy with staff meetings and planning of events." The First Lady's role is the epitome of what sociologist Hanna Papanek calls the "two-person career"— that combination of "formal and informal institutional demands placed on a married couple" by reason of the husband's career. The contributions that wives in these careers make include "status

maintenance, intellectual contributions, and public performance."
In terms of public performance, the First Lady functions as representative of the nation. She welcomes heads of state, presides at
state dinners, makes public appearances in person and through
the media, attends local and national celebrations, and becomes
the patroness of selected charities. These aspects of the role can
be compared to the duties assumed by royal families. Eleanor
Roosevelt used the parallel with royalty in a letter to Jackie Kennedy:
"To smile no matter how weary one is, to look well-dressed and
interested at all times is a remarkable feat, especially when it is
considered that we do not have the long training given to royalty
to meet these situations."

In terms of status maintenance and intellectual contribution,
the First Lady is expected to be a kind of national wife—the
embodiment of American womanhood (an ideal that evolved
throughout the nineteenth century). The modern office of First
Lady differs markedly from that of the nineteenth century. Then,
as historian Barbara Welter has observed, the First Lady's principal
duties were social, not political. Even the social obligations were
regarded as onerous by some first ladies, who avoided them by
claiming invalidism (then a perfectly acceptable excuse for not
going out in society) or religion. Rachel Jackson[1] and Eliza Johnson claimed the latter, and a long list of first ladies, from Elizabeth
Monroe and continuing through Lucy Hayes, retreated to the
upper floor of the White House as invalids. As to intellectual contribution, Welter has commented that although nearly every president talked politics to his wife, "there has been a tendency on the
part of biographers to discount completely any role or influence
of the wife."

The emphasis on social aspects tended to enforce a uniformity
of public behavior on the various women who played the role,
and this was true up to and through the presidency of Herbert
Hoover. First Lady Lou Henry Hoover was, in the White House, "a
far cry," notes Welter, "from the tomboy Lou Henry who majored
in geology at Stanford, an extraordinary thing for a woman to do,
who translated the de re metallica from the Latin, and bicycled
through the Chinese Revolution amid spraying bullets, and single-
handedly organized a committee to return 10,000 Americans
from overseas." Lou Hoover's personality became submerged in
the role she played as the president's wife, a role still defined by

---

[1] Rachel Jackson died before her husband Andrew was inaugurated in 1829.

the outworn norms of the previous century. What made Lou Hoover's position especially poignant, however, was that women's position in society had changed.

In the early nineteenth century, Alexis de Tocqueville[2] had observed the fact, puzzling to him, that American women, unlike European women, seemed to disappear from the public scene once they married. This resulted partly from the patriarchal repressiveness of the Puritan heritage in early America, but also from the overwhelming responsibilities that women bore in the home. For Charles Wilson Peale, portraitist to the elite of the young country and a typical eighteenth-century generalist, marriage was "a social bond . . . by which harmony, industry and the wealth of the nation are promoted." According to his biographer, Peale was convinced that the family circle provided the moral education of the next generation, where were taught "discipline, balance, duty and benevolence; virtues highly important to the young American republic." His thinking was typical of the times. Even Abigail Adams's famed plea to her husband to "remember the ladies" and grant them rights of citizenship was argued on the assumption that the "ladies" were responsible to society as mothers and educators of men.

By the 1840s, this theory of the female role was expanding to include realms beyond the home. Strong-minded women of the time felt the contradiction between the subordination of women and the ideals of a nation that prided itself on its democratic spirit. Educator Catharine Beecher (sister of Harriet Beecher Stowe), for example, thought of women as teachers to the nation and tried to reconcile their patently inferior position by elevating the tasks they performed. In a sense, Beecher took Peale one step further, by ascribing to women a central moral and educative role not only in the family but in a web of institutions that included the family, the school, the church. Women, she argued, should function as exemplars and teachers of a national morality both at home and in the classroom, both privately and publicly. As the century progressed, women became the civilizing and community-building force on frontier after frontier and the moving force behind the abolition and temperance movements.

By the turn of the century, a combination of education and zeal for uplift and reform blossomed into the formation of women's associations and the establishment of such organizations as settlement houses. Professionalized social work and prison work were

---

[2] Tocqueville, a French aristocrat, visited and wrote about the United States in the 1830s.

added to the "traditional" women's occupations of nursing and teaching. The "Lady Bountiful" charitable enterprises of upper- and middle-class women were becoming quasi-professional volunteer activities in the service of organizations like the Red Cross and the Junior League.

Eleanor Roosevelt, sixteen years old when the century turned, conformed to this emerging ideal of woman. She had been prepared by her education at Allenswood to enter activities that would improve the world. As a debutante, she took up volunteer work that exposed her to social conditions demanding reform. As a young wife, she was active in the Consumers' League, the Women's Trade Union League, and the League of Women Voters.

She became a practical politician and party worker, not only in behalf of her disabled husband, but because of her own interests. As she wrote in a League of Women Voters' bulletin: "On the whole the Democratic Party seems to have been more concerned with the welfare and interests of the people at large, and less with the growth of big business interests. . . . If you believe that the people must struggle slowly to the light for themselves, then it seems to me that you are logically a Democrat."

Last of all, she had been the very active First Lady of the largest state in the union. She came to the White House with a lively sense of the people, of their variety, of their needs, and of what government could do to change their lives.

Of all the first ladies, then, Eleanor Roosevelt had the most complete preparation for the role in all its aspects. In addition to being from a family established in New York society, she was also from a presidential family, Her consciousness of what a first family could be must have been affected by her closeness to the family of her uncle, President Theodore Roosevelt. Studies have shown that women of achievement are often influenced by the strong male role models in the family—if not a father (which was sadly unlikely in Eleanor Roosevelt's case), then a brother or other close relative. As a young woman, she must have seen that the White House was indeed, as Theodore Roosevelt put it, "a bully pulpit."

Theodore Roosevelt's presidency has been characterized as the first media presidency; Eleanor Roosevelt became the first media First Lady. She gave women journalists a status and opportunity they had not previously enjoyed by holding her own press conferences, restricted to them, and dispensing hard news at these conferences so that newspapers and syndicates had to add women to their staffs. "But it was not just that she legitimized them as journalists," says Doris O'Donnell, daughter of Doris Fleeson, one of the columnists closest to ER, but that she made them part of what was going on. It was in the Roosevelt administration that the press—largely writing press then—became part of the establishment—literally the fourth estate. The age of the muckrakers was over for the moment. Just as the president legitimized the press by establishing regular press conferences, so did 'Mrs. R.' as the press women called her. But I think there was a difference.

The difference, as O'Donnell sees it, lay in the fact that, in befriending the press, FDR skillfully used journalists for his purposes (and for the best interests of the nation, as he saw those interests). Through them, through the control of information and access, he had a tool with which to confound his enemies. "Mrs. Roosevelt used them too," says O'Donnell,

> but in a very different way. She enlisted them in her causes. She had an extraordinary creative capacity to see how people could best use their talents. These women had fought their way to the top in their professions against great odds. Some of them were hard-bitten. They were not easily taken in. But they responded to Mrs. Roosevelt's vitality, sincerity, strength of character and her real interest in them.

* * *

In much the same way as she was able to enlist journalists, Eleanor Roosevelt was to enlist labor leaders, educators, women in government, and youth leaders. By the time she reached the White House, she had long since learned to reach across all barriers to create friendships, whether with a Kansas populist like Doris Fleeson or a black leader like Mary McLeod Bethune. "No head of state was received like Mrs. Bethune," wrote J. B. West, White House usher; "Mrs. Roosevelt would run down the drive to meet her and they would walk up the drive arm in arm."

With Eleanor Roosevelt as chatelaine, the White House became the symbol of the inclusiveness of true democracy. She was prodigiously hospitable. "It seems that there were never less than twenty for lunch," says J. B. West. In her autobiography, *This My Story,* she lists those entertained in one year: over four thousand for lunch, more than nine thousand for tea, and others for dinner almost every night when she was not traveling. Undoubtedly, she began inviting people in numbers in order to bring the world to a stricken husband, but by the time of the height of her activities as First Lady her hospitality had become a means of catalysis, of bringing people together for their mutual benefit and to further the causes she believed in.

* * *

The change, however, was not immediate, although Roosevelt obviously entertained the hope that other first ladies would use the "office" as she had. One of her first acts after the President's death was to offer to introduce Bess Truman to "the girls" of the press corps, at what she assumed would be the latter's first press conference. According to Frances Perkins, the new First Lady was filled with trepidation at the prospect. Perkins advised her that if she didn't want to have press conferences there was no need to have them—that she thought there was no precedent for doing so other than that set by Eleanor Roosevelt, who was a special case. Whether thus persuaded or not, Bess Truman never did hold a press conference and left relations with the press to her highly respected social secretary, Edith Helm.

Bess Truman and Mamie Eisenhower preferred to restrict their activities to providing companionship to their husbands and acting as White House hostesses—almost in the mold of the nineteenth-century first ladies. They were both of Roosevelt's generation but lacked her background for translating social and official position into opportunities to affect the common good. Nor, it would seem, had they a desire to do so.

Presidents Kennedy and Johnson and their staffs seem to have recognized, in the expansion of and emphasis on the First Lady's office, a way of giving an added dimension to their administrations. Jacqueline Kennedy's choice of staff was at least approved in the West Wing, both President Johnson and Elizabeth "Liz" Carpenter have told of Johnson's summoning the latter to his office and telling her to "get over there and help Lady Bird." Each First Lady added something to the public role. Jacqueline Kennedy became the first First Lady to lead an official commission. Lady Bird Johnson's "beautification" project, despite the somewhat gimmicky tone of its title, bore real results by calling attention to the environment and improving the quality of life in towns and cities, especially Washington, D.C. The so-called Billboard Bill, abolishing commercial advertising signs along highways built with federal money, was passed with her support (and with some presidential arm-twisting in Congress).

By the time Pat Nixon entered the White House, the pattern was set. The question was not whether she would have a project but what her project would be. Her choice of using her official status to call attention to "voluntarism" was innocuous and in the good Republican tradition of de-emphasizing government aid.

But it must be remembered that she was also the first First Lady to be sent to a foreign country as personal representative of the president during peacetime. Betty Ford set out to emphasize the arts but, almost by accident, became an exponent of feminism and a sponsor of the Equal Rights Amendment, although her sponsorship was largely a public relations effort that had little practical political effect.

Rosalynn Carter quite deliberately set out to emulate Eleanor Roosevelt. She sensed, it would seem, that she had to make an overt effort to rescue the "office" of the First Lady from mere celebrity-hood and the appearance of influence. Her insistence on regular office hours and on having a business lunch with the president on a weekly basis, like his other advisers, was part of this effort. But her lack of a Washington base and a limited rapport with the press—a radically different press corps in the post-Watergate era than that dealt with by First Ladies Kennedy, Johnson, and even Nixon—brought the effort little success.

Her failure points to a basic difficulty in what has come to be the establishment of a quasi-official office, that of First Lady. Hanna Papanek expressed it well:

> The limits to acceptable participation by the wife in the husband's public image are illustrated by those cases where the wives become public personalities themselves and no longer operate only in the context of the husband's role. The key expression which indicates that these stereotyped limits have been exceeded is the statement "she is a . . . in her own right."

Other difficulties inherent in the increasingly public role of the office are illustrated in the experience of Eleanor Roosevelt. First of all, the public side of her life often curtailed the private satisfactions of family life, a fact she recognized. In her autobiography she wrote that "public life is fine for one's ideals but it is very high in personal sacrifice. No matter what happens I do not think a woman ever feels the loss in personal relations is compensated for."

Secondly, although Roosevelt was better equipped than some of her successors to deal with the fact, she depended heavily on the press, especially the women of the press. It can even be said they made use of her to call attention to conditions that interested them, and to reach the president. In some sense they "made" her, even as she "made" them. Anne Cottrell Free, who was one of the younger reporters admitted to the group close to Mrs. Roosevelt, has noted with some disapproval that they protected her. "There was a great deal of hinting and prompting at those press conferences," she told a seminar on first ladies at Hunter College in

1982. "'Are you sure you want to say that, Mrs. Roosevelt?'
'Wouldn't you like to say this, Mrs. Roosevelt?' It wasn't exactly
objective journalism."

In 1933, within weeks of moving into the White House, ER
demonstrated the revolutionary nature of her interpretation of
the role of First Lady. Commentator Heywood Brown, who was a
successful playwright himself, wrote that he for one was "delighted
we are going to have a woman in the White House who feels like
Ibsen's Nora,[3] she is before all else a human being and that she
has a right to her own individual career." It was obvious to many
Americans that this was a new kind of First Lady.

But it might be best to let ER herself tell about those precedent-
setting days of 1933, as she recalled them in her *Autobiography*.

ELEANOR ROOSEVELT'S ACCOUNT OF HER FIRST YEAR IN THE WHITE HOUSE

From the time we moved to Washington in 1933, Louis Howe
became more and more of an invalid. At first he was able to be
in his office and to keep his finger on much that was doing on,
and the second bonus march[4] on Washington by the veterans of
World War I he handled personally.

The first march, which had taken place in Mr. Hoover's administration, was still fresh in everybody's mind. I shall never forget
my feeling of horror when I learned that the Army had actually
been ordered to evict the veterans from their encampment. In the
chaos that followed, the veterans' camp on the Anacostia flats
was burned and many people were injured, some of them seriously. This one incident shows what fear can make people do, for
Hoover was a Quaker, who abhorred violence, and General
MacArthur, his chief of staff, must have known how many veterans would resent the order and never forget it. They must have
known, too, the effect it would have on public opinion.

---

[3] Ibsen's play, *A Doll's House*, featured a woman named Nora who chose her own
dreams over the requirements of a conservative society.
[4] World War I veterans, suffering from the Depression's economic reversals, marched
to Washington to demand early benefits from the bonus Congress had promised
them in 1924.

When the second bonus march took place in March of 1933 I was greatly worried for fear nothing would be done to prevent a similar tragedy. However, after talking the situation over with Louis Howe, Franklin immediately decided that the veterans should be housed in an old camp and provided with food through the relief administration. Louis spent hours talking with the leaders. I think they held their meetings in a government auditorium and were heard by the proper people in Congress. As a result, everything was orderly.

Although Louis often asked me to take him for a drive in the afternoon, I was rather surprised one day when he insisted that I drive him out to the veterans' camp just off Potomac Drive. When we arrived he announced that he was going to sit in the car but that I was to walk around among the veterans and see just how things were. Hesitatingly I got out and walked over to where I saw a line-up of men waiting for food. They looked at me curiously and one of them asked my name and what I wanted. When I said I just wanted to see how they were getting on, they asked me to join them.

After their bowls were filled with food, I followed them into the big eating hall. I was invited to say a few words to them—I think I mentioned having gone over the battle fronts in 1919—and then they sang for me some of the old army songs. After lunch I was asked to look into several other buildings, and finally we came to the hospital that had been set up for them.

I did not spend as much as an hour there; then I got into the car and drove away. Everyone waved and I called, "Good luck," and they answered, "Good-by and good luck to you." There had been no excitement, and my only protection had been a weary gentleman, Louis Howe, who had slept in the car during my entire visit.

* * *

The President's wife does not go out informally except on rare occasions to old friends. Now and then, in the spring, Elinor Morgenthau[5] and I stole away in my car or hers, and stopped in at some little place for lunch or tea. Driving my own car was one of the issues the Secret Service people and I had a battle about at the very start. The Secret Service prefers to have an agent go with the President's wife, but I did not want either a chauffeur or a Secret Service agent always with me; I never did consent to having a Secret Service agent.

---

[5] Wife of Henry Morgenthau, FDR's Secretary of the Treasury.

After the head of the Secret Service found I was not going to allow an agent to accompany me everywhere, he went one day to Louis Howe, plunked a revolver down on the table and said, "Well, all right, if Mrs. Roosevelt is going to drive around the country alone, at least ask her to carry this in the car." I carried it religiously and during the summer I asked a friend, a man who had been one of Franklin's bodyguards in New York State, to give me some practice in target shooting so that if the need arose I would know how to use the gun. After considerable practice, I finally learned to hit a target. I would never have used it on a human being, but I thought I ought to know how to handle a revolver if I had to have one in my possession.

Always, when my husband and I met after a trip that either of us had taken, we tried to arrange for an uninterrupted meal so that we could hear the whole story while it was fresh and not dulled by repetition. That I became, as the years went by, a better reporter and a better observer was largely owing to the fact that Franklin's questions covered such a wide range. I found myself obliged to notice everything. For instance, when I returned from a trip around the Gaspe, he wanted to know not only what kind of fishing and hunting was possible in that area but what the life of the fisherman was, what he had to eat, how he lived, what the farms were like, how the houses were built, what type of education was available, and whether it was completely church-controlled like the rest of the life in the village.

When I spoke of Maine, he wanted to know about everything I had seen on the farms I visited, the kinds of homes and the types of people, how the Indians seemed to be getting on and where they came from.

Franklin never told me I was a good reporter nor, in the early days, were any of my trips made at his request. I realized, however, that he would not question me so closely if he were not interested, and I decided this was the only way I could help him, outside of running the house, which was soon organized and running itself under Mrs. Nesbitt.

In the autumn I was invited by the Quakers to investigate the conditions that they were making an effort to remedy in the coal-mining areas of West Virginia. My husband agreed that it would be a good thing to do, so the visit was arranged. I had not been photographed often enough then to be recognized, so I was able to spend a whole day going about the area near Morgantown, West Virginia, without anyone's discovering who I was.

The conditions I saw convinced me that with a little leadership there could develop in the mining areas, if not a people's revolution, at least a people's party patterned after some of the previous parties born of bad economic conditions. There were men in that area who had been on relief for from three to five years and who had almost forgotten what it was like to have a job at which they could work for more than one or two days a week. There were children who did not know what it was to sit down at a table and eat a proper meal.

One story which I brought home from that trip I recounted at the dinner table one night. In a company house I visited, where the people had evidently seen better days, the man showed me his weekly pay slips. A small amount had been deducted toward his bill at the company store and for his rent and for oil for his mine lamp. These deductions left him less than a dollar in cash each week. There were six children in the family, and they acted as though they were afraid of strangers. I noticed a bowl on the table filled with scraps, the kind that you or I might give to a dog, and I saw children, evidently looking for their noonday meal, take a handful out of that bowl and go out munching. That was all they had to eat.

As I went out, two of the children had gathered enough courage to stand by the door, the little boy holding a white rabbit in his arms. It was evident that it was a most cherished pet. The little girl was thin and scrawny, and had a gleam in her eyes as she looked at her brother. She said, "He thinks we are not going to eat it, but we are," and at that the small boy fled down the road clutching the rabbit closer than ever.

It happened that William C. Bullitt was at dinner that night and I have always been grateful to him for the check he sent me the next day, saying he hoped it might help to keep the rabbit alive.

This trip to the mining areas was my first contact with the work being done by the Quakers. I liked the theory of trying to put people to work to help themselves. The men were started on projects and taught to use their abilities to develop new skills. The women were encouraged to revive any household arts they might once have known but which they had neglected in the drab life of the mining village.

This was only the first of many trips into the mining districts but it was the one that started the homestead idea. The University of West Virginia, in Morgantown, had already created a committee to help the miners on the Quaker agricultural project. With that committee and its experience as a nucleus, the government obtained the loan of one of the university's people, Mr. Bushrod Grimes, and established the Resettlement Administration. Louis

"For gosh sakes, here comes Mrs. Roosevelt!"
Robert Day © 1933 from The New Yorker Collection. All rights reserved.

Howe created a small advisory committee on which I, Mr. Pickett, and others served. It was all experimental work, but it was designed to get people off relief, to put them to work building their own homes and to give them enough land to start growing food.

It was hoped that business would help by starting on each of these projects an industry in which some of the people could find regular work. A few small industries were started but they were not often successful. Only a few of the resettlement projects had any measure of success; nevertheless, I have always felt that the good they did was incalculable. Conditions were so nearly the kind that breed revolution that the men and women needed to be made to feel their government's interest and concern.

I began to hear very serious reports of conditions in Logan County, West Virginia, where for many years whole families had been living in tents because they had been evicted from company houses after a strike. All the men had been blacklisted and could not get work anywhere; they were existing on the meager allowance that the State of West Virginia provided for the unemployed. Now the tents were worn out, illness was rampant, and no one had any medical care. Finally Mrs. Leonard Elmhirst[6] and I established a clinic to take care of the children. When I told my husband of the conditions there he said to talk to Harry Hopkins[7] and to tell him that these families must be out of tents by Christmas. It was done, and for two years, out of my radio money and Mrs. Elmhirst's generosity, we tried to remedy among the children the effects of conditions which had existed for many years.

I came to know very well a stream near Morgantown called Scott's Run, or Bloody Run, because of the violent strikes that once occurred in the mines there. Some of the company houses, perched on hills on either side of the run, seemed scarcely fit for human habitation. The homestead project started near Morgantown was called Arthurdale and took in people from all the nearby mining villages.

One of the first people to go to Arthurdale was Bernard M. Baruch,[8] who helped me to establish the original school and always took a great interest in the project, even visiting it without me on some occasions. I have always hoped that he got as much satisfaction as I did out of the change in the children after they had been living on the project for six months.

The homestead projects were attacked in Congress, for the most part by men who had never seen for themselves the plight of the miners or what we were trying to do for them. There is no question that much money was spent, perhaps some of it unwisely. The projects were all experimental. In Arthurdale, for instance, though the University of West Virginia recommended the site, apparently nobody knew what was afterwards discovered—that there was a substratum of porous rock which finally caused great expense in making the water supply safe. Nevertheless, I have always felt that many human beings who might have cost us thousands of dollars in tuberculosis sanitariums, insane asylums, and jails were restored to usefulness and given confidence in themselves. Later, when during World War II, I met boys from that area I could not help thinking that a great many of them were

---

[6] A philanthropist and friend of Eleanor.

[7] Hopkins directed FDR's Federal Emergency Relief Administration and later the Works Progress Administration.

[8] In World War I Bernard Baruch directed the War Industries Board.

able to serve their country only because of the things that had been done to help their parents through the depression period.

Nothing we learn in this world is ever wasted and I have come to the conclusion that practically nothing we do ever stands by itself. If it is good, it will serve some good purpose in the future. If it is evil, it may haunt us and handicap our efforts in unimagined ways.

Years later, after the Social Security Act[9] was passed, I saw how it worked in individual cases in this area. There was a mine accident in which several men were killed, and my husband asked me to go down and find out what the people were saying. One man received the Carnegie medal posthumously[10] because he had gone back into the mine to help rescue other men. His widow had several children, so her social security benefits would make her comfortable. In talking to another widow who had three children and a fourth about to be born, I asked how she was going to manage. She seemed quite confident and told me: "My sister and her two children will come to live with us. I am going to get social security benefits of nearly sixty-five dollars a month. I pay fifteen dollars a month on my house and land, and I shall raise vegetables and have chickens and with the money from the government I will get along very well. In the past probably the mine company might have given me a small check and often the other miners took up a collection if they could afford it, but this income from the government I can count on until my children are grown."

Two other events of that first autumn in Washington stand out in my mind. On November 17, 1933, Henry Morgenthau, Jr., was sworn in as undersecretary of the treasury in the Oval Room in the White House, thus starting on his long and arduous labors in the Treasury Department. When Secretary Woodin resigned, Henry Morgenthau succeeded him and held the office until shortly after my husband's death, when he also resigned and left Washington.

On that same day my husband and Mr. Litvinov[11] held the final conversations on the recognition of the Soviet Union. There was considerable excitement over the first telephone conversation between the two countries which took place between Mr. Litvinov in the White House and his wife and son in Russia. The ushers noted it in their daily record book because, while there had been

---

[9] The Social Security Act of 1935 was an insurance program to help children, the elderly, and the disabled.

[10] An award given by the estate of philanthropist Andrew Carnegie.

[11] Maxim Litvinov was in 1933 the Soviet Union's foreign minister.

overseas conversations with many other European countries, this was the opening of diplomatic relations with Russia.

Needless to say, among some of my husband's old friends there was considerable opposition to the recognition of Russia. His mother came to him before the announcement was made to tell him she had heard rumors that he was about to recognize Russia, but that she felt this would be a disastrous move and widely misunderstood by the great majority of their old friends.

Not only his old friends but with various other people my husband had frequent run-ins over the new theory that government had a responsibility to the people. I remember that when Senator Carter Glass insisted that Virginia needed no relief, Franklin suggested that he take a drive with him to see some of the bad spots. The senator never accepted his invitation.

The opening of diplomatic relations with Russia and our relations in this hemisphere were the administration's first points of attack in our foreign policy, but the major emphasis in those early years was and had to be on questions of domestic policy and our internal economic recovery.

As I look back over the actual measures undertaken in this first year I realize that the one in which my husband took the greatest pleasure was the establishment on April 5, 1933, of the Civilian Conservation Corps camps. The teen-age youngster, the boy finishing high school, the boy who had struggled to get through college, were all at loose ends. There was no organization except the Army that had the tents and other supplies essential for a setup of this kind, which was why part of the program was promptly put under its jurisdiction.

Franklin realized that the boys should be given some other kind of education as well, but it had to be subordinate to the day's labor required of them. The Civilian Conservation Corps had a triple value: it gave the boys a chance to see different parts of their own country, and to learn to do a good day's work in the open, which benefited them physically; also it gave them a cash income, part of which went home to their families. This helped the morale both of the boys themselves and of the people at home. The idea was his own contribution to the vast scheme of relief rehabilitation planning.

This was followed on June 16 by the National Recovery Act, with General Hugh Johnson in charge. The basic importance of the NRA was that it made it easier for the industrialist who wanted to do the right thing. The chiseler and the man who was willing to profit by beating down his labor could no longer compete unfairly with the man who wanted to earn a decent profit but to treat his employees fairly. The NRA was declared unconstitutional almost two years later. I thought this was unfortunate, for it seemed a simple way to keep bad employers doing what was right.

The Public Works Administration, which came into being on the same day, made it possible for the government to plan and undertake public works during this period of depression. It helped to take up the slack of unemployment by lending money to the states for projects that they could not finance by themselves.

Five months later, in November, 1933, the Civil Works Administration was set up and in time put four million unemployed to work.

In my travels around the country I saw many things built both by PWA and by CWA. I also saw the results of the work done by CCC. The achievements of these agencies began to dot city and rural areas alike. Soil conservation and forestry work went forward, recreation areas were built, and innumerable bridges, schools, hospitals and sanitation projects were constructed—lasting monuments to the good work done under these agencies. It is true they cost the people of the country vast sums of money, but they did a collective good and left tangible results which are evident today. They pulled the country out of the depression and made it possible for us to fight the greatest and most expensive war in our history.

Perhaps the most far-reaching project was the Tennessee Valley Authority. That was Senator George Norris' greatest dream and no one who witnessed the development of the Authority will ever forget the fight he put up for something that many people ridiculed. The development had been begun during World War I, but at the end of that war most of the work was stopped. Nothing further was done until my husband, who understood Senator Norris' vision, supplied the impetus at a time when it could accomplish the maximum results for the country. With the demands of a possible war in mind, Franklin insisted on pushing work on the TVA as rapidly as possible. He believed even then that under certain circumstances war might come soon, and he knew if that happened we would need everything the TVA could make available.

In the campaign of 1932 my husband and I had gone through some of the TVA area, and he had been deeply impressed by the crowds at the stations. They were so poor; their houses were unpainted, their cars were dilapidated, and many grownups as well as children were without shoes or adequate garments. Scarcely eight years later, after the housing and educational and agricultural experiments had had time to take effect, I went through the same area, and a more prosperous region would have been hard to find. I have always wished that those who oppose authorities to create similar benefits in the valleys of other great rivers could have seen the contrast as I saw it. I realize that such changes must come gradually, but I hate to see nothing done. I wish, as my husband always wished, that year by year we might be making a start on the Missouri River and the headwaters of the Mississippi. Such experiments, changing for the better the life of the people, would be a mighty bulwark against attacks on our democracy.

Almost from the time FDR was inaugurated in March 1933, ER assumed the role of a "New First Lady." She became the President's eyes and ears and reported to him the conditions she found on her visits to troubled places. She freely offered advice on policy and programs for relief. She started relief projects on her own. She observed federal programs and provided FDR with evaluations of their effectiveness.

COMMENTS ON HER ROLE BY LORENA HICKOCK, FRANCES PERKINS, AND HELEN GAHAGAN DOUGLAS

Three women, Lorena Hickock, Frances Perkins, and Helen Gahagan Douglas, had opportunity to observe ER as she began her role as First Lady and continued to perform them for over twelve years. Together they explain her interests, her goals, and her methods. We begin with the comments of ER's personal friend and adviser Lorena Hickock:

She had not been in Washington a month before she was assigned to do one of those reporting jobs her husband had trained her to do. A second bonus march had brought more penniless veterans of World War I streaming into Washington, desperately demanding immediate payment. But this time there was no need for them to build a ramshackle camp on Anacostia Flats like the one the Army had burned the summer before. President Roosevelt had an old Army camp just outside Washington opened up for them and directed the Relief Administration to supply them with food. And then, of course, he had to know how they were getting along. So out to the camp one afternoon, driving her own little blue convertible and accompanied only by Louis Howe, went his wife to find out for him.

Thus began a twelve-year series of "go and see" journeys that were to carry her back and forth and up and down the country into places never before visited by anyone from the White House. To Scott's Run and the worked-out mines in West Virginia. Down into a coal mine in southern Ohio. To the cardboard shacks of the "Okies" along the irrigation ditches in California. To cutover timberlands, where unemployed city men were trying to learn to be farmers. To the Dust Bowl, where the wind blew the top soil into piles like black snowdrifts along the fences. To Puerto Rico and the Virgin Islands, to wartime Britain and Guadalcanal. Not one of those trips did she make without the approval of her husband. The journeys to Britain and the Pacific were made at his request. He encouraged her to go out on her lecture trips, for they paid her expenses. Assuming that she got them only because she was the President's wife, she did not regard her enormous earnings as her own property and gave them away. One year she had to dip into her modest capital, her share of her parents' estate, to pay her income taxes. Someone finally convinced her that she could with propriety accept the checks herself, hold out enough to cover the taxes, and forward the balance to the American Friends, the Red Cross and the other beneficiaries, instead of having them turned over in full as she had been doing!

Mrs. Roosevelt does not believe she had any influence in the formation of her husband's policies. But a government policy under our system must be based on the needs and wishes of the people. Never was there a President who knew so much about what was happening to the people of this country and what they thought about it as the man they elected to the office four times. Nobody else could have done for him what she did. He used to say that one of the difficulties of a President was that nobody told him the truth. Either they were so awed by the fact that he was President that they "yessed" him, or they had angles of their own to play and told him only what they wanted him to hear. His wife did not "yes" him, and she had no angles to play. He frequently did not agree with her conclusions and always made up his own mind, but she gave him the facts more objectively and more honestly than anyone else could have given them to him.

In political matters, Mrs. Roosevelt says she had little influence with her husband and never tried to have any. She very likely had more than she thinks, but her natural inclination would have been to refrain from offering him advice, for she had a great deal of confidence in his political judgment and little in her own. His sense of timing, she says, was a gift she did not possess and never acquired. When she saw a thing to be done, her impulse was to go ahead and do it immediately, disregarding obstacles that would certainly impede her progress and might stop her completely. He would bide his time wait patiently for the right moment, look for cracks in the wall or ways around it before he went charging into it. His was the better way, she acknowledges, although she found it exasperating. Nor would she have tried to meddle in his political career any more after he became President than she had before.

Frances Perkins, a former social worker who was Secretary of Labor from 1933 to 1945, remembered FDR's reaction to the role ER played, a role she had established during the 1920s, both in their private life and in public affairs:

> The President was enormously proud of her ability, although he rarely talked about it except to someone in whose sympathy he felt complete confidence. He said more than once, "You know, Eleanor really does put it over. She's got great talent with people." In cabinet meetings he would say, "You know my Missus gets around a lot," or "my Missus says that they have typhoid fever in that district," or "my Missus says the people are leaving the dust bowl in droves because they haven't any chances there," or "My Missus says that people are working for wages way below the minimum set by NRA[12] in the town she visited last week."
> He had complete reliance in her observations. He often insisted on action that public officials thought unnecessary because Mrs. Roosevelt had seen with her own eyes and had reported so vividly that he too felt he had seen. They were partners.

And Helen Gahagan Douglas, the California actor turned social activist who was a Roosevelt partisan throughout FDR's presidency and a friend to ER until her death, recalls the way ER planned the many White House dinners so as to encourage progressive thought and action:

---

[12] The National Recovery Act of 1933 created the National Recovery Administration, which set minimum wage standards for the country.

It always seemed to me that Mrs. Roosevelt invited her guests with one thought in mind—to cross-fertilize creative energies.

Like a bird-dog, she spotted persons she believed were doing or would do important work. She recognized, encouraged, praised, and helped them. Workers in big jobs, little jobs, in and out of government, rural and city folk—they all became her friends. She saw to it that they became her husband's friends. Before the war, she brought them to meet him—as many and as often as the President's schedule would permit. They were invited to come and dine with him and, in their own words, tell him of their work.

There would be a mixed gathering. There might be several old friends; neighbors from Hyde Park like the Henry Morgenthaus; some member of the large Roosevelt family; Harry Hopkins, the President's aide, who lived in the White House; an obscure expert on a subject of current concern; a specialist from one of the bureaus; and very, very often there would be a newcomer Mrs. Roosevelt had spotted—someone who had never been in the White House before.

These dinners were all so graciously and gracefully managed that one had no sense of being educated.

Mrs. Roosevelt guided the conversation. The guests were in her hands, even the President followed her lead. Mrs. Roosevelt was in complete command, though it wasn't to herself that she drew attention, but to her husband.

One was aware at all times that Eleanor Roosevelt was the wife of Franklin Roosevelt. She addressed him as Franklin and referred to him as Franklin. She was at one and the same time intimate, informal, and natural with him, yet one was aware of her respect, even in her informality, of the office of the presidency and the person of the President.

Dinner would start gaily. The President and Mrs. Roosevelt would keep the conversation easy, light, bouncy. The President might question Mrs. Roosevelt about something she had been doing—might even good-naturedly bait her a bit.

When Mrs. Roosevelt believed that the newcomer's first self-consciousness had passed, that he had recovered from the shock of being where he was, she would draw the President's attention to him. "Franklin," she would say, "Mr. X is doing such interesting work. Mr. X, won't you tell Franklin about it?"

The President would smile, approve, question, make suggestions. He might recall that similar work was going on in another state or point out where it was needed. And then the conversation would become general. And the new friend, who never in his wildest dreams thought he would be sitting where he was, conversing naturally with the President of the United States, basking in the interested-in-him atmosphere Mrs. Roosevelt had created, would feel at ease and return home to work harder than ever. For some, this contact with the President at the White House resulted in the course of their lives being changed, in sacrifices never intended to be made. The President and Mrs. Roosevelt's zest for their own work was contagious.

General awareness of the President and Mrs. Roosevelt's receptivity to information brought a stream of voluntary reports from the forty-eight states. The President was reached through his wife. Visitors, messages, mail connected millions of people to the capital. And so it was that Eleanor Roosevelt flung wide the doors of the White House.

Mrs. Roosevelt went out of the White House to meet the many who would never come to Washington—who would never see the White House.

I shall never forget the scene in late 1939 of Mrs. Roosevelt standing among migrant workers in the fields of California, as much at home as in a drawing room at the White House, as gracious as though greeting an ambassador.

Mrs. Roosevelt was coming to our state to give a number of lectures. I wanted her to see firsthand the plight of the farm migrants who were living on the ditch banks of California, to compare that with life in Farm Security camps. There were a number of government farm camps in the San Joaquin Valley, but many more were needed. I hoped the administration would build them.

Hundreds of thousands of little farmers, sharecroppers, tenant farmers, and farm hands were on the road. Tens of thousands were coming into our state. Federal and state governments were hard put to cope with these rootless folk.

Californians took sides as to what should be done. In our state, the farm migrants became a subject of fierce contention. Many farmers saw them only as more hands, a cheaper supply of labor—while many city taxpayers saw them only as an unwelcome financial burden to be got rid of quickly. And if that wasn't possible, to ignore them, deny they were there.

The migrants needed everything: clothes, food, medicine, work, a place to live. The condition of the migrant children was pitiful. In addition to everything the government was doing, volunteer help was needed and welcomed. I arranged with Mrs. Roosevelt to visit the San Joaquin valley. Her schedule, as usual, was very tight, but I hired a plane to squeeze out two hours for the visit.

After landing in the valley, we set out in cars, escorted by Farm Security officials. As we drove down the country road on the way to the first camp, Mrs. Roosevelt spotted a cluster of makeshift houses made of boards, tarpaper, and old tin cans hammered flat. Some men were working in the field, farm migrants who had their first toehold on a piece of earth in their new state.

"Stop the car, please," said Mrs. Roosevelt—and with that, she was out and walking briskly into the fields. I followed as quickly as I could.

One of them men straightened to see who was coming and instantly stepped forward. With hand outstretched and beaming face, he greeted the First Lady with these words: "Oh, Mrs. Roosevelt, you came to see us."

This farm migrant and the others with him thought it perfectly natural that she should be there. They were not at all surprised to see her in their field.

After a few minutes' chat, Mrs. Roosevelt made for one of the shacks.

"Please don't go in there, Mrs. Roosevelt. My wife and children are all sick with the chicken pox."

"It doesn't matter," she replied—and in she went.

AN ASSESSMENT OF ELEANOR ROOSEVELT'S ROLE AS SOCIAL REFORMER FIRST LADY, BY TAMARA HAREVEN

ER changed not just the style of First Lady; she changed the substance as well. It was not enough for her—and future First Ladies—merely to be; they also had to do. ER wanted to do nothing less than reform the nation. She went among the people, she used her prestige to tackle problems, she spoke her mind, she used the mass media to communicate her concerns, her ideas, her hopes and dreams. She helped create the American mind. In the following essay, continuing her comments from the Part I on ER's preparation to be a reformist First Lady, scholar Tamara Hareven assesses the way ER used her position as First Lady to lead social reform:

Eleanor Roosevelt felt [in 1933] an era was coming to an end. Often before, she had expressed apprehension about the changes that were taking place in American society; the general instability, the erosion of family autonomy, the impersonality of life in large cities, the restlessness, the endemic poverty and unemployment even during prosperity. But she had never anticipated such a crisis. Now it reverberated up and down the land.

Mainly under the impact of the depression, Eleanor Roosevelt came to look at economic security as the indispensable pillar of democracy. She defined economic security as an economic level "below which no one is permitted to fall, and keeping a fairly stable balance between that level and the cost of living." Her definition included the right of a laborer to a useful and remunerative job, of a farmer to a fair return for his produce, of a businessman to protection from unfair competition, of every family to a decent home, and of every person to adequate care, proper education, and provision for old age.

Further, the Great Depression taught her that equality of opportunity meant more than an "honest broker" government; it meant constructive aid to underprivileged groups and a social and economic system that would guarantee their individual rights. The government had to undertake the positive role of furthering social justice and guaranteeing minimum economic security. . . . When Eleanor Roosevelt arrived in the White House in 1933, she was already an experienced politician and a committed social reformer. But she had no clear plan. In her energetic plunge into new activities as First Lady, Roosevelt dramatized and advertised the mood of the early New Deal: frantic action, readiness to experiment, concern for the "forgotten man," and a realistic recognition of the grimness of the social problems of the depression, accompanied by a faith in combating them.

Though she initially viewed her role as that of auxiliary to her husband, Roosevelt also started to work independently for the causes she deemed important. In the beginning, she did not plan her course. She picked up new causes as they came along. "Somebody asked me to 'come and let us show you what is happening here,' and, being interested, I went. Then another invitation came, and I went. And each thing I saw proved so fascinating I found myself going more and more, farther and farther." Quickly, however, she developed the mechanisms for investigating social problems on a human level, established channels of direct communication between the general public and the White House, and developed her own role as intermediary between the New Deal and the public and between New Deal administrators and the president. She developed the power inherent in the position of First Lady into a unique instrument for furthering social reform.

In sustaining this role, the First Lady had several advantages. Unconstrained by any official administrative position, she could speak out more freely than could the president. She had access to New Deal agencies through their heads and administrators. From the beginning of the New Deal, administrators turned to her for help and contact with the president; gradually, she took the initiative and sent them her queries, criticisms, and advice. Because of her influence, even those who felt uneasy about her interference continued to appeal to her when they needed her support. Even her enemy and public critic, Westbrook Pegler, recognized the emergence of a reform agenda in the First Lady's activities: "Mrs. Roosevelt has been too busy with such trivialities as old-age pension, a ban on child labor, and the protective health of mothers and children," he wrote in his column on April 25, 1935.

Roosevelt's support of New Deal relief and reform programs reflected her concern with the welfare of individuals, as well as with larger social problems. Her efforts to build lasting social reform elements into temporary relief measures and her campaigns for the launching of far-reaching reforms, such as social security or fair labor standards, had an important effect on the shaping of the New Deal's reform agenda that went beyond emergency measures and helped lay the foundation for the welfare state.

As First Lady, her attitude toward relief agencies revealed a skillful combination of reformer and politician. On the one hand, she tried to supervise the administration of the various relief agencies and to see that they had an impact at the grass-roots level. At the same time, she tried to construct elements of permanent social reform rather than view New Deal measures strictly as temporary measures.

During the "First Hundred Days" of the New Deal, Eleanor Roosevelt began to assume new responsibilities. She was concerned that, in the rush and excitement accompanying the launching of new projects, human dignity should not be sacrificed to administrative expedience. The New Deal should not defeat its purpose by overlooking the needy groups that had been habitually ignored —single women, youth, blacks, and sharecroppers. At the same time she sought a rational administration of work relief, with a view to the needs of communities and an emphasis on productive employment rather than "busywork."

In the complex administrative machinery of government relief, Eleanor Roosevelt occupied the unique role of intermediary between the average person and the government. People in trouble, encouraged by her public invitation to write about their problems, called for help. In addition, she developed the practice of forwarding the letters requesting help to the National Democratic Committeewoman in the state from which the letter came. The committeewoman took the case to the appropriate relief agencies.

In her concern for the "forgotten" in American society, Eleanor Roosevelt went beyond her Progressive predecessors and pushed the New Deal's relief programs and reform measures to encompass the groups that had been previously left out. She focused on the establishment of relief agencies for women and youth and emphasized equal treatment for blacks. . . . She quickly and effectively helped launch special programs for unemployed women. By December 17, 1933, about 100,000 women were among the 2,610,451 workers under the FERA and the Civil Works Administration (CWA). Thirty-five states appointed women directors to head work projects for women. At ER's insistence, Hopkins issued recommendations to include women wherever possible in the reemployment program. He suggested that they be given clerical jobs, even if this meant transferring men from such positions to other jobs. In this case and others in the 1930s, Eleanor Roosevelt's advocacy of women was motivated not as much by feminism as by her quest for social justice.

✳ ✳ ✳

The breadth of Roosevelt's relief concerns, particularly her commitment to folk culture and to the popularization of the folk arts, was expressed in her support of the WPA's writers and arts projects. She supported these efforts out of sympathy for unemployed artists and writers, a lively interest in the development of a national style, and a desire to stimulate the public's receptiveness to the arts. Experimenting with government patronage of the arts was particularly appealing to her because it carried a potentially lasting impact.

The arts and writers' projects also appealed to her sense of history and tradition. She saw these projects as the cultural counterpart of soil conservation and reforestation—an effort to preserve national resources. It was an expression of the rediscovery of common people, a new interest in their welfare, lives, and culture, as an important part of American culture. Roosevelt became progressively more convinced of this parallel. ER supported the collection of information on cities and whole regions for local guides (information that might otherwise have been lost to posterity), the preservation of historical documents, and the microfilming of old newspapers. The WPA Writers' Project amassed huge collections of folklore, slave narratives, local guides, and the Index of American Design which were all part of this effort.

Roosevelt's populist view of the arts was also expressed in her support of the WPA's Theater and Arts projects. Rather than turn the White House into a bastion of high culture, she supported the traveling concerts and "Caravan Theater" projects, for people who had never had the opportunity to see the theater or the arts:

> Last year, and I imagine we will find this duplicated this year, the average weekly audience of these Caravan Theaters were over 500,000 people. These plays are given free, of course, and for this reason many people who have never been able to, see and attend.
>
> Somehow we must build throughout this country a background of culture. No nation grows up until that has been accomplished, and I know of no way which will reach more of our people than the great plays of the past and present authors.

Although Roosevelt rarely agreed to assign a rank to the projects she was supporting, her commitment to black equality took a high place. From the 1930s on, the rights of blacks emerged as one of her major causes. She began to advocate the urgency of fighting discrimination long before the race riots of the 1940s brutally awakened many Americans to this necessity and long before "civil rights" had become a central reform issue. She was the only one in the New Deal administration to express an active interest in blacks and to take a personal and semiofficial stand on civil rights, even when she risked antagonizing political support for the president.

The development of Eleanor Roosevelt's stand on racial discrimination parallels the changing emphases within the civil rights movement itself. She began by addressing whites and blacks in different terms. To white audiences she emphasized that discrimination was primarily a moral issue, which endangered the very fiber of American society. Although ER attacked inequality in a general way, she specifically distinguished between political and legal inequality on the one hand and social inequality on the other. She admitted that progress toward a voluntary social acceptance of blacks as equals would be slow, because it was impossible for any government to dictate it; it could develop only as people progressed spiritually. The government, however, had to remove all legal barriers, ensure equality in the courts and in employment, and prevent limitations being placed on people "except such as may be imposed by their own character and intelligence."

When addressing blacks, however, Roosevelt talked in the Booker T. Washington[13] tradition. She stressed that blacks had to be as much responsible for their fate as whites and called on them to be practical and to develop their abilities and skills within the existing social framework. She urged them to compromise and use a "certain amount of intelligence in trying to fit the person who is capable of doing, to the job he can get." In answer to the question whether the federal government had any responsibility for the existence of separate lockers and lunchrooms in federal buildings in Washington, Roosevelt said diplomatically, "I think the federal government is established in a city which is still largely a Southern city. Now, like it or not, we cannot change things in a day." However, she was less compromising on the rights of black labor. When the minimum wage was introduced, and employers decided that if they had to pay a minimum of fourteen dollars a week, they would rather pay it to white workers than to blacks, Eleanor Roosevelt stated emphatically: "It is a question of the right to work, and the right to work should know no color lines."

As on other reform issues, Roosevelt fought segregation and discrimination by setting a personal example, anticipating much of the activism of the Civil Rights movement of the 1960s. In 1938, while attending the Southern Conference for Human Welfare in Birmingham, Alabama, she saw the delegates seated in two separate rows according to color. She took a seat on the side marked "Colored" and refused to move to the "White" side. When police threatened to break up the meeting, she reluctantly took her chair to the platform facing the audience, but placed it closer to the blacks' side. On that occasion, however, she was bolder in her conduct than in her public statement. When asked later by newspapermen for her opinion of the Alabama segregation law, she controlled her indignation and said that it was "a question for Alabama to decide." Moreover, by 1940 she had not yet mentioned desegregation in educational institutions, housing, and public service as major goals of civil rights.

Eleanor Roosevelt thus used the New Deal's framework to benefit blacks by concentrating on the development of segregated employment opportunities, proper housing, education, and med-

---

[13] Washington founded Tuskegee Institute for blacks in 1881 and led it until his death in 1915. He stressed the need for black Americans to help themselves rather than wait for white largess.

ical care. Soon after her arrival in Washington in 1933, she started her campaign for the liquidation of the alley dwellings in Washington, most of which were black ghettos. Following the pragmatic spirit of the New Deal, she seized upon the opportunity provided by its various agencies to try and achieve equality for blacks within those relief agencies, particularly in the NYA. Though the New Deal did not deliberately take the initiative on legislative reforms for desegregated equality, it at least offered blacks an opportunity to benefit from the general improvement of social and economic conditions, in which they shared with other depression-stricken groups.

To her credit, after all this legislation passed in the "First Hundred Days," Eleanor Roosevelt warned that the New Deal was still far from meeting its major goals. And throughout her White House years, she remained both the New Deal's advocate and its critic. After her husband's death in 1945, she lost her unique power position and her role of protector, but remained active in the public arena and continued to defend the New Deal's reform tradition as a "private citizen." Now she idealized it and made its principle the yardstick of all government policies. She realized that new problems had to be met with new answers, as long as the New Deal's principles were maintained. As the living symbol of the New Deal, she carried political power. Reform organizations courted her approval, and candidates in the Democratic party sought her endorsement. However, she identified the Democratic party with the reform tradition, and as the New Deal's custodian she refused to allow opportunists to use the New Deal as a slogan to further their own interests.

During the 1930s black Americans, who had traditionally been supporters of the Republican Party because of its association with Lincoln, moved in large numbers toward the Democrats because of the Roosevelts, particularly because of ER. In her book *Farewell to the Party of Lincoln,* Nancy Weiss documents the effect FDR's New Deal had on black political attitudes and commitments; and she points specifically to ER's influence in forging a lasting bond between black America and the Democratic Party, despite the fact that the New Deal helped blacks little.

She also demonstrates the irony that ER, with all her outward and doubtlessly sincere efforts to help blacks, was at heart a typically aristocratic white woman. Although she was sensitive to the plight of blacks and believed deeply in justice and decency, she seemed also to believe in gratitude. Weiss quotes ER acquaintance Kenneth Clark: "She believed that blacks should be grateful. I never had the feeling, as much as I liked her, that she really understood the fundamental social, ethical, moral aspects of the problem. I think she was much more sentimental about it."

Still, she was concerned, and she more than anyone in FDR's circle called the nation's attention to racial—as well as social, economic, and gender—injustice. The television character of the 1970s, Archie Bunker, once commented on the popular satirical comedy *All in the Family* that no one knew there were any "coloreds" in America "until Eleanor Roosevelt discovered 'em." In this and many other ways ER used her place as First Lady to create the modern American mind.

A TRIBUTE FROM HILLARY RODHAM CLINTON

Hillary Rodham Clinton, while in many ways very different from Eleanor Roosevelt, is the First Lady most often compared to her. Mrs. Clinton, the wife of a felicitous and earnest political leader who craves public approval as did FDR and who admittedly also has a least once turned to a woman of less commanding intelligence for female companionship, has said that at times she has felt she is following in ER's footsteps, both publicly and personally. After a trip abroad in 1995, she wrote the following tribute to ER in her weekly syndicated column:

> One thing I've learned since becoming First Lady is that wherever I go, Eleanor Roosevelt has surely been there before me.
>
> I've been to farms in Iowa and factories in Michigan where Mrs. Roosevelt paid a visit a half century ago. I've been to schools and colleges named for Mrs. Roosevelt and walked the halls of hospitals she toured before I was born.
>
> Even when I go to other countries, Mrs. Roosevelt has doubtless been there first. When my daughter and I went to Pakistan and India last spring, we discovered that Eleanor Roosevelt had traveled there in 1952, and even had written a book about her trip.
>
> Now I'm in South America, following in Mrs. Roosevelt's footsteps yet again. She came here several times and visited several countries, sharing her vision of justice and compassion with all

who would listen. The United States, she believed, had a vested interest in helping any neighbor in our hemisphere that sought to build a democratic way of life.

"Our obligation to the world is primarily our obligation to our own future," she once said. "Obviously, we cannot develop beyond a certain point unless other nations develop, too."

Traveling now through South America, I find myself thinking often about Mrs. Roosevelt—who was born 111 years ago October 11. And I'm convinced that if she were still alive today, nothing would thrill her more than coming to watch children perform at the Circus School in Brazil.

It's a place I'm visiting on this trip where runaway children learn the principles of discipline and teamwork, and build self-confidence through acrobatics and trapeze training. Not only do these children show a renewed interest in education and improved attendance in school, they perform before sellout crowds every weekend.

Mrs. Roosevelt also would be right at home chatting with the poor women I met at a neighborhood center in Santiago, Chile, or listening to women in Managua, Nicaragua, talk about the sewing business they started with $100 loans from the local bank and support from the U.S. government.

Wherever she went, Mrs. Roosevelt celebrated the richness of the human experience. She appreciated every person's potential to do something great with very little. Perhaps that is why people all over the world, including here in South America, remember her with such admiration and fondness.

QUESTIONS FOR RESPONSIVE ESSAYS

1. What personal experiences in ER's life helped make her the activist First Lady of the New Deal era? How might another woman have used some of these same experiences to present a completely different image and act in a completely different way?

2. How did her training in public affairs during the 1920s, particularly the "networking" she had done with like-minded women, prepare ER for the role she began to play in 1933 as First Lady? Without such training how might she have acted differently and less effectively?

3. How did the events of her first year in the White House and her reactions to them set the pattern for her twelve years as First Lady? Why was the reaction to her at the same time so positive among some Americans and so negative among others? In what ways did she strengthen and in what ways might critics say she weakened the office of First Lady?

4. What made Eleanor Roosevelt "without precedent" as First Lady? What new things did she do, and how did she do them? In what ways did she change the role of First Lady forever? In what ways have First Lady Hillary Rodham Clinton and other First Ladies since World War II been like First Lady Eleanor Roosevelt, and in what ways have they been different from her?

5. What kind of social reformer was Eleanor Roosevelt? What did she want to see reformed in American society, and how did she use her position as First Lady to accomplish those reforms? What would a First Lady of more conservative philosophy and/or temperament have tried to accomplish during the Depression? How would one of more radical philosophy and/or temperament have gone further than she did?

PART III

First Lady of the World

We can establish no real trust between nations until we acknowledge the power of love above all other power.

—ELEANOR ROOSEVELT
This Troubled World, 1938

She never regarded communism as the primary enemy. Poverty, ignorance, discrimination, the denial of civil liberties, the failure to act and think with independent judgment—those were the primary enemies.

—BLANCHE WIESEN COOK
Without Precedent, 1984

ELEANOR ROOSEVELT AND WORLD WAR II (1941–1945)

For most of FDR's first two terms as President (1933–1941) ER concerned herself with domestic issues. She strongly supported her husband's New Deal programs to stimulate the economy and end the Great Depression. Her own hopes and programs for American social reform were often more radical and progressive, particularly in civil and women's rights, than those of her more pragmatic husband. But toward the end of the 1930s, as war loomed both in Asia and in Europe, she turned her attention more and more to world affairs. She did not abandon her concerns for social justice; she merely expanded her field of vision.

She had all of her adult life been, both privately and publicly, a pacifist. She did not believe war to be a solution to disagreements among nations. But when war with fascist nations became apparently inevitable, she changed her mind and her position. Fascist governments around the world not only challenged America's security, but by their racism and chauvinism they threatened the very rights she had worked so hard to achieve. She first encouraged Americans to develop civil defenses; and then after America entered the war following the bombing of Pearl Harbor in 1941, she wholeheartedly supported the war effort. In the process, through her travels, she became a world figure in her own right.

As she had served as FDR's eyes and ears and legs, and even his voice, while he confronted the challenge of the Depression, now she served in the same ways as he confronted the challenge of World War II. She went on fact-finding missions during the war to England, the South Pacific (including Australia), and the near west. In all of these places she conferred with national leaders, visited American troops on training bases and in hospitals, and encouraged the participation of women in war enterprises. The following passage from her autobiography describes the kind of experiences she had during her second wartime trip in 1943. She shows great concern for the soldiers and deep interest in the contribution women were making. She doubtless conveyed both to FDR when she returned.

Having told the story of my two trips to parts of the world where actual war was going on and where, of necessity, one saw the results of the war in the hospitals, I think I should say something of the impressions these trips left with me.

At first I could hardly bear the hospitals. There was, of course, a certain amount of pure physical fatigue from walking miles of hospital wards day after day; but that was nothing in comparison with the horrible consciousness of waste and feeling of resentment that burned within me as I wondered why men could not sit down around a table and settle their differences before an infinite number of the youth of many nations had to suffer.

The most horrifying hospitals were those in which the men who had been mentally affected by the experiences they had been through were treated. I could tell myself, of course, that these men would probably have broken under other circumstances, that there must be something wrong with our civilization when our young people were so vulnerable to mental illness and that we must work to discover the reasons and try to change them; nevertheless, my horror at seeing people who had broken mentally and emotionally made me lie awake nights.

ER hosting U.S. soldiers at a White House garden party during World War II

There were times in the other hospitals when it was hard to accept the gallantry of the men themselves without showing how deeply sorry I was for them. I knew that was the last thing they wanted and that their brave front of casual cheerfulness was put on to prevent people from showing that they were sorry.

Many of the boys I saw in hospitals are now leading happy and useful lives, but they carry with them, day after day, the results of the war. If we do not achieve the ends for which they sacrificed— a peaceful world in which there exists freedom from fear of both aggression and want—we have failed. We shall not have paid our debt until these ends are achieved.

One development gives me great hope for the future. Women have always come to the fore in wartime, but I think in World War II they took responsibility in more fields than ever before—in factories, on the farms, in business, and in the military services. They were an indispensable part of the life of the country. This was true in Great Britain, in Australia, in New Zealand, in France, in all occupied countries in Europe, in Russia, and in the United States. Women have become conscious also of the need to take part in the political life of their country. In the European countries more women are today playing an active role in public life than would have been possible before the war; and I am sure we are going to see great developments in the Asiatic area too. This, to me, is a hopeful sign, for women will work for peace as hard as they worked for the war.

HER OWN ACCOUNT OF HER YEARS AT THE UNITED NATIONS (1946–1952)

Eleanor Roosevelt's life as First Lady of the United States ended in April 1945, after twelve years as America's most prominent woman, when FDR died in his fourth term as President. He died at his resort in Warm Springs, Georgia, with Lucy Mercer at his side, ER at work in Washington. World War II was drawing to an end, and so it appeared was ER's public life. She still felt strongly about domestic and foreign affairs. She wanted New Deal reform to continue to provide a better standard of living to poor Americans. She wanted legislation passed that would ensure racial equality. She wanted Nazism rooted out of Europe and continued cooperation with wartime allies, including the Soviet Union, enhanced. Yet now she had, or so she thought, no forum for her views.

Little did she know that a new chapter in her public life was just beginning, one in which she would earn by her hard, persistent labor the title "First Lady of the World."

The new U.S. President, Harry Truman, appointed her to a five-person delegation to the January 1946 London Conference on the United Nations. Several U.S. Senators, remembering that on social matters, particularly civil rights, she was even more liberal than FDR had been, opposed her nomination. In the end, though, only Mississippi Senator Theodore Bilbo voted against her. Two of her fellow delegates, Republicans John Foster Dulles and Arthur Vandenburg, made no effort to hide their feeling that she was too liberal and too naive to take on foreign affairs in the tough new postwar world.

But she went to London and proved herself well-prepared for her duties and capable of handling the challenges of the new *realpolitik.*[1] She later called her work with the United Nations the "most wonderful and worthwhile experience in my life." In an effort to consign her to work that would not entail dealing with sensitive political or economic matters, considered man's work, Eleanor was appointed to Committee Three, the group that would deal with humanitarian, cultural, and educational matters. The first issue to come before Committee Three was the problem of war refugees.

Because she considered the work she did at the United Nations so significant in her life, Eleanor devoted a great deal of space to it in her autobiography. Here are memories of the way she began:

> I drove to the first session of the General Assembly in London with Mr. Stettinius, who was then assistant secretary of state, accompanied by Mr. Sandifer[2] and two other young advisers. Each delegate had a desk and there were several seats behind him for his advisers. The gathering of so many representatives of the large and small nations was impressive.
>
> The first business of the Assembly was concerned with organization and the election of the first president, Paul-Henri Spaak of Belgium, a wonderful diplomat, an eloquent orator and a statesman of stature who did much to help the United Nations get off to a good start. The first Secretary General of the United Nations was Trygve Lie, a Norwegian. He was an able man who strongly believed in the ideas behind the United Nations, which he served well. He was a positive personality, which possibly was a handicap in his position, for he eventually made enemies. It is important that the Secretary General not only should be a good negotiator but should be able to make practically everyone feel he is their friend—if such a thing is possible.
>
> At the early sessions in London I got the strong impression that many of the old-timers in the field of diplomacy were skeptical of the new world organization. They had seen so many failures, they had been through the collapse of the League of Nations, and they seemed to doubt that we would achieve much. The newcomers

---

[1] A term used since the time of Germany's Bismarck to describe foreign policy based on self-interest and the use of power.
[2] Durward Sandifer served as Eleanor's political adviser during her time at the United Nations.

were the ones who showed the most enthusiasm and determination. They were, in fact, often almost too anxious to make progress. It was fortunate that such men as Mr. Spaak and Mr. Lie were on hand and skillful enough to give the veterans new inspiration and to hold the newcomers in check when necessary.

During the entire London session of the Assembly I walked on eggs. I knew that as the only woman on the delegation I was not very welcome. Moreover, if I failed to be a useful member, it would not be considered merely that I as an individual had failed but that all women had failed, and there would be little chance for others to serve in the near future.

I tried to think of small ways in which I might be more helpful. There were not many women on the other delegations, and as soon as I got to know some of them I invited them all to tea in my sitting room at the hotel. About sixteen, most of them alternate delegates or advisers, accepted my invitation. Even the Russian woman came, bringing an interpreter with her. The talk was partly just social but as we became better acquainted we also talked about the problems on which we were working in the various committees. The party was so successful that I asked them again on other occasions. I discovered that in such informal sessions we sometimes made more progress in reaching an understanding on some question before the United Nations than we had been able to achieve in the formal work of our committees.

As a result, I established a custom, which I continued throughout the years I was connected with the United Nations, of trying to get together with other nations' representatives at luncheon or dinner or for a few hours in the evening. I found that often a few people of different nationalities, meeting on a semisocial basis, could talk together about a common problem with better results than when they were meeting officially as a committee.

As time went on, there were more and more women serving on various delegations, and ours usually had a woman alternate even while I was still a delegate. Helen Gahagan Douglas, Mrs. Ruth Bryan Rohde, and Edith Sampson all were extremely valuable on the United States delegation.

As a normal thing the important—and, I might say, the hard—work of any organization such as the United Nations is not done in the big public meetings of the General Assembly but in the small and almost continuous meetings of the various committees. In the committee meetings each nation is represented by one delegate or an alternate and two or three advisers.

The discussions and the compromises and the disagreements that occur in committee meetings are of utmost importance.

At first I was not familiar with committee work and not sure of myself, but Mr. Sandifer was always seated just behind me to give me guidance. As time went on I got so I could tell merely by his reactions whether the discussion was going well or badly. If I could feel him breathing down my neck I knew that there was trouble coming, usually from the Russians.

There is a question many people have asked me about the responsibilities of a delegate to the United Nations. "You are representing your government, but do you do exactly what you are told to do or say? Do you have any latitude for self-expression or for personal judgment in voting?"

The answer is a little complicated. In the first committee meetings I attended in London I was in complete agreement with the position of the State Department on the question at issue: the right of war refugees to decide for themselves whether they would return to their countries of origin. I was uncertain about procedure, however, and often lagged behind when the chairman called for a vote. Finally, Mr. Sandifer said sternly:

"The United States is an important country. It should vote quickly because certain other countries may be waiting to follow its leadership."

After that I always tried to decide how I would vote before a show of hands was asked for and, as soon as it was, my hand went up with alacrity. In deciding how to vote, it is true that a delegate, as a representative of his government, is briefed in advance on his country's position in any controversy. In London, fortunately, I agreed with the State Department position. But later I learned that a delegate does have certain rights as an individual and on several occasions I exercised my right to take a position somewhat different from the official viewpoint.

Of course, a delegate cannot express his disagreement publicly unless he resigns, since obviously it would be impossible to have representatives of the same nation saying different things in the United Nations. But he may exercise his right to disagree during the private briefings. Before the start of a session we were told what subjects would be on the agenda. If you disagreed with the government's attitude you had the right to say so and to try to get the official attitude changed or modified. You could, if necessary, appeal to the President to intervene and you could, if there was no solution, resign in protest.

On one occasion I did object vigorously to our official decision to rescind, without explanation to our people, the position we had taken on recognizing the Franco government in Spain.[3] I was joined by other delegates and the State Department put off action until it could explain the situation fully.

The first issue to come before Committee Three was the problem of refugees, persons displaced from their homes by the war, many of them afraid to return for fear of being punished for leaving, afraid of the governments that controlled their homelands. In the following passage from her memoirs, ER recalls how she battled the Soviet representative Andrei Vishinsky over this issue:

It was while working on Committee Three that I really began to understand the inner workings of the United Nations. It was ironical perhaps that one of the subjects that created the greatest political heat of the London sessions came up in this "unimportant" committee to which I had been assigned.

The issue arose from the fact that there were many displaced war refugees in Germany when the Armistice was signed—Ukrainians, Byelorussians, Poles, Czechoslovaks, Latvians, Lithuanians, Estonians, and others—a great number of whom were still living in temporary camps because they did not want to return to live under the Communist rule of their own countries. There were also the pitiful Jewish survivors of the German death camps.

The Yugoslav and, of course, the Soviet Union position, put forth by Leo Mates,[4] was that any war refugee who did not wish to return to his country of origin was either a quisling[5] or a traitor. He argued that the refugees in Germany should be forced to return home and to accept whatever punishment might be meted out to them.

The position of the Western countries, including the United States, was that large numbers of the refugees were neither quislings nor traitors, and that they must be guaranteed the right to choose whether or not they would return to their homes. I felt strongly on the subject, as did others, and we spent countless hours trying to frame some kind of resolution on which all could

---

[3] Generalissimo Francisco Franco led Spain's fascist government, which survived the fall of Hitler in Germany and Mussolini in Italy.

[4] Yugoslav representative to the UN, who followed Soviet lines of reasoning.

[5] A quisling is someone who sells out his own country in order to be the puppet of a foreign occupying army. The word comes from Vidkun Quisling, who served the Nazis as head of the puppet government during the occupation of Norway.

agree. We never did, and our chairman, Peter Fraser of New Zealand, had to present a majority report to the General Assembly, which was immediately challenged by the U.S.S.R.

In the Assembly the minority position was handled by Andrei Vishinsky, one of Russia's great legal minds, a skilled debater, a man with ability to use the weapons of wit and ridicule. Moscow considered the refugee question of such vital importance that he spoke twice before the Assembly in a determined effort to win over the delegates to the Communist point of view. The British representative on our committee spoke in favor of the majority report. By this time an odd situation had developed. Someone would have to speak for the United States. The question threw our delegation into a dither. There was a hurried and rather uncomfortable consultation among the male members and when the huddle broke up John Foster Dulles approached me rather uncertainly.

"Mrs. Roosevelt," he began lamely, "the United States must speak in the debate. Since you are the one who has carried on the controversy in the committee, do you think you could say a few words in the Assembly? Nobody else is really familiar with the subject."

I said I would do my best. I was badly frightened. I trembled at the thought of speaking against the famous Mr. Vishinsky. Well, I did my best. The hour was late and we knew the Russians would delay a vote as long as possible on the theory that some of our allies would get tired and leave. I knew we must hold our South American colleagues until the vote was taken because their votes might be decisive. So I talked about Simon Bolivar and his stand for the freedom of the people of Latin America. The South American representatives stayed with us to the end and, when the vote was taken, we won.

This vote meant that the Western nations would have to worry about the ultimate fate of the refugees for a long, long time but the principle of the right of an individual to make his own decisions was a victory well worthwhile.

Toward the end of the sessions we worked until late at night. The final night the vote on Committee Three's report was taken so late that I did not get back to the hotel until about one o'clock. I was very tired, and as I walked wearily up the stairs at the hotel I heard two voices behind me. Turning around, I saw Senator Vandenberg and Mr. Dulles.

"Mrs. Roosevelt," one of them said, "we must tell you that we did all we could to keep you off the United Nations delegation. We

begged the President not to nominate you. But now we feel we must acknowledge that we have worked with you gladly and found you good to work with. And we will be happy to do so again."
I don't think anything could have made the weariness drop from my shoulders as did those words. I shall always be grateful for the encouragement they gave me.

A CONTEMPORARY WOMAN'S IMPRESSION OF ELEANOR ROOSEVELT AT THE UNITED NATIONS

The various UN sessions and committee meetings were held in an ever-changing set of locales, but ER remained steadfastly committed to her crusade for human rights. Elizabeth Janeway, who wrote the following article for the *New York Times Magazine,* captured her in the early stages of her work, when her committee was meeting in Lake Success, Long Island, New York. Janeway admitted that at first she was a bit put off by ER's shyness and her giggle but that once she saw her fierce determination she was impressed:

> Mrs. Roosevelt is the chairman of the Commission on Human Rights whose work on a draft covenant is to be considered by Committee Three. This is a body appointed by the Economic and Social Council of the U.N. (Not to be confused with UNESCO, which is a separate but affiliated body with its own delegates.) The first duty of the commission was to draw up a Declaration of Human Rights, and this it has done. After some two years of struggling over the principles of contemporary ethics and the minutiae of wording, the Universal Declaration of Human Rights was accepted by the General Assembly in December, 1948. The principles of the declaration have already borne fruit, for both the Indian and Indonesian Constitutions have modeled themselves after it, and it has been referred to in decisions by the Federal courts of the United States.
>
> This, then, is Mrs. Roosevelt's biggest job: to bring down to earth the ideals of the Declaration of Human Rights and contrive, by the lengthy process of discussion and compromise, by bickering and by vote, to get them woven by her committee into an implementation which will be accepted by the United Nations as a whole and by each of the nations singly.
>
> At her job she is untiring. When she first sat as chairman of her commission, she was unfamiliar with parliamentary procedure and was inclined to think common sense an adequate substitute

for Robert's "Rules of Order." This was a naive, if good-hearted view. She has since got over it and is quite capable of quoting the procedural rules of the United Nations from memory.

She quoted them last spring with great firmness to Mr. Tsarapkin, the Russian delegate, who appeared briefly at the first meeting of the session of the Human Rights Commission.

It was Mr. Tsarapkin's not unexpected desire to have the delegate from Nationalist China expelled and a representative of the Chinese Communist Government seated in his place. Mrs. Roosevelt ruled that he could present his resolution only on a point of order, which she then overruled on the grounds that, since Dr. Chang had been confirmed in his place by the Economic and Social Council, he could be removed only by this body and not by the Human Rights Commission itself.

She quoted to Mr. Tsarapkin the rule by which he could appeal to a majority of the commission to overrule the chairman's decision. The vote sustained her, and Mr. Tsarapkin, who consistently addressed Mrs. Roosevelt as "Mr. Chairman," launched into a passionate oration. This accused the Nationalist Chinese of numerous crimes, the American Government of aiding and abetting them, and Mrs. Roosevelt specifically of using her position as chairman of the group for political purposes.

In the middle of this denunciation Mrs. Roosevelt's gavel came down with a crack, and it was seen that she could lose her temper with great effect. "I am sorry, sir," she said. "We are now going to proceed with the election of officers. This is no place for propaganda speeches and I must ask you to draw your remarks to a close."

The formality of her speech was matched by the fury in her voice. Then, in a moment or two, she regained her composure and, on Mr. Tsarapkin's request, allowed him to continue to the end, when he and his Ukrainian colleague walked out.

At the General Assembly Mrs. Roosevelt is able to divide the work to be covered at this session with the distinguished Negro lawyer, Mrs. Edith Sampson, who is also a delegate to Committee Three. Still, the volume of what she must get through is enormous. Mrs. Sampson herself says that she has learned from Mrs. Roosevelt the techniques of concentration and of programming that enable her to handle her responsibilities.

In the daily meetings of the United States delegation Mrs. Roosevelt does not confine her attention to questions before Committee Three. She is *au courant* with the problems of the Budgetary, Economic, and Political Committees and does not hesitate to comment upon them.

These "briefing" sessions take place before and after meetings, and Mrs. Roosevelt's day will often include a morning session at the United States delegation's offices in New York, continuing in the delegation car on the way to Lake Success, two commission meetings at U.N. headquarters and further discussion in the late afternoon before she goes to a dinner, where she is likely to speak on her work at the United Nations.

Nor are her lunch hours periods of relaxation. The U.N. staff, which used to assemble in awe to watch her pass in the corridor, has got used to seeing her hurry into the delegates' lounge, drop a stuffed briefcase on the most convenient chair and plunge on through toward the cafeteria where she stands in line to be served, holding her own try and waiting her turn. Then, if she has time, she will return to the lounge (she has no other office at Lake Success) to meet and talk to a group of students or the members of some organization before the afternoon meeting of the commission. Now that she has added a daily radio program to her schedule, her closest friends are awestruck at the scope of her activities.

This is part and parcel, however, of what she considers a vital part of her job. She is out to cure the country, so far as it is humanly possible for her to do so, of its ignorance about the United Nations and particularly about the great question of human rights. The indefatigable energy which sent her, when she was First Lady, down mines and into hospitals now dispatches her to every speaking engagement she can manage to squeeze in. Convinced, devoted, tireless, endlessly available, she is a symbol of hope for progress throughout the world.

She does not particularly like to be a symbol and, indeed, denies that she is one in her own right. "All that," she says, with a touch of embarrassment and distaste at the mention of her prestige, "all that is because people associate with me what my husband meant to them." For herself, if her work could be done as effectively without it, she would be glad to dispense with any symbolic value she may have in the world's eyes.

Mrs. Roosevelt not only believes that privilege is morally wrong; she actively dislikes to be, herself, in a privileged position. Such a feeling is sometimes confused with modesty, or even humility, but it is in truth something much closer to pride; to the kind of pride which believes that using advantages is a sign of weakness, and that to start even with the world and still win out is the greatest achievement possible to a privileged person.

Not that Mrs. Roosevelt denies the usefulness of prestige. She has not always agreed with the instructions from Washington to the United States delegation, and she has carried her arguments to the Secretary of State and to the President on more than one occasion. When she arrived in Paris for the General Assembly late in 1948 she discovered that the United States position on Spain was one with which she disagreed. She presented her arguments against a softening at the time of our attitude toward France with great cogency. Senator Austin reported them to the American Government and the United States position returned to its original stiffness.

She is alert, too, to the uses of the advisers who sit behind her at meetings. Soviet Foreign Minister Vishinsky once launched into a lengthy speech which included a listing of what he described as American concentration camps. Mrs. Roosevelt noted them down and handed the list to one of her aides who rushed out to phone Washington. By the end of Mr. Vishinky's oration Mrs. Roosevelt had a report from the Army on the locations mentioned—which had been prisoner-of-war camps, most of them closed.

In her own commission she has used a simple maneuver to cut down the length of speeches. "Have you ever noticed," she will remark with an air of ingenuousness to a long-winded speaker, "about when it is that people begin to remove their headphones? It takes about ten minutes of any speaker's time." Yet her attitude in the chair is one of generous encouragement. "Yes? Yes?" She will say, as if this at last—whatever the subject, whoever the speaker—were bringing her final clarification. "I felt as if she had been waiting all day for me to speak," one delegate said.

The Russians, of course, with their invective, their accusals and their stereotyped denunciations, are a special problem: By the end of the 1949 session of the Commission on Human Rights Mrs. Roosevelt had more or less worked out a basic formula for dealing with them. Whenever she could ignore the rhetoric and charges with which they prolonged the debate she did so, and spoke merely to the point of whatever their actual suggestions for the drafting of the Covenant might be. She had certainly begun her work at the U.N. by attempting to meet the Soviet delegates halfway, but by 1949 she was ready to state publicly that she would never again try to compromise with them.

As for the Soviet Government itself, it had definitely changed its expressed opinion of Mrs. Roosevelt. The Russians began by calling her nothing worse than a "school teacher" (she replied that she was proud to be regarded as a member of the teaching profession), and even two years ago they were willing to appeal to her, in the name of her husband, to cease advocating "imperialism." Such temperance has stopped, however, and *Izvestia* later referred to her as a "hypocritical servant of capitalism . . . a fly darkening the Soviet sun." In Paris, late in 1948, a Russian delegate was heard to mutter some words in the heat of debate which seemed to characterize Mrs. Roosevelt as a meddling old woman. An observer was forcefully reminded of Stalin's projected plan for dealing with Lenin's widow, Krupskaya. That unhappy lady was more inclined to Trotsky's view than to Stalin's and for some little time made no bones about saying so. "If that old woman doesn't shut up," Stalin is said to have remarked, "I'll appoint someone else Lenin's widow." There is no doubt he would like to have the power to appoint someone else Franklin D. Roosevelt's widow.

Actually Mrs. Roosevelt herself is undoubtedly pleased to have Mrs. Sampson, a younger woman, associated with her and has said that eventually she must withdraw. But in the meantime she must speak for the United States in Committee Three and on the Human Rights Commission. This is not always simple. As United States delegate, of course, she must always remember those operative words, "two-thirds of the Senate." A covenant on human rights which is not ratified by the United States Senate will not be a covenant at all, either to America or, practically speaking, to the world at large. No one west of the Iron Curtain can doubt Mrs. Roosevelt's firm adherence to the humanitarian statements of the Declaration of Human Rights. But it is just this adherence to principle which makes her advocate practical compromise.

The United States point of view has thus far excluded from the Covenant of Human Rights economic and social rights, such as the promise of unemployment insurance or material benefits. It has, moreover, restricted very sharply the bringing of petitions for redress against violators of the covenant. Such petitions cannot be presented by distressed individuals, or by organizations representing them, no matter how large a group the organization represents. They can be brought only by national Governments signatory to the covenant.

This puts a wronged human being, whether he be a Czech Democrat, a South African Negro, or a California Japanese subject to the Alien Land Law, in the position of having to discover another national Government willing to bring a case in his behalf against his own Government. To many, such restrictions seem to narrow the covenant to farcical limits; and worse, to invite the bringing of cases as political propaganda. Why does Mrs. Roosevelt support such a position?

Mrs. Roosevelt recognizes both the force and familiarity of this criticism. But she replies on pragmatic grounds. If individual, or even organizational, petitions were permitted, she says, any apparatus for dealing with violations under the covenant would be swamped. "As it is," she points out, "we have letters from people complaining about their rent being raised."

Mrs. Roosevelt goes on to say that she sees this covenant as a first covenant; as a step to be taken so that more can follow. Let us get this covenant ratified—and here the words "two-thirds of the Senate" almost appear in the air over her head—let us take this first step, and then we can go on to work on covenants which can include social and economic rights; to plan for the acceptance first of organizational petitions and then of individual pleas.

Thus she and her critics meet head-on in this ancient philosophic dilemma of ends and means. Mrs. Roosevelt is for means, of the pragmatic approach so typical of American thought. She is for action. Let us do as much as we can, she believes, and, if we cannot do all we want at once, what we do will be better than nothing. Surely we can win the trust of the oppressed millions of the world by honest effort in their behalf, even though our accomplishments at first must be disappointing.

In the formulation of public policy Mrs. Roosevelt will never play the role of Caesar's wife and be content to keep herself above criticism by folding her hands and sitting still; and to expect her to prefer her value as a symbol above the human effort of hands, heart and head is to misjudge her entirely. She is at bottom an optimist who believes that "there can be an infinite variety of methods, but the objective everywhere is the same. How can you build a world in which all men get a chance of full development of themselves as individuals, and for a better surrounding in which to achieve that end?"

It is because she is an optimist that she is willing to move slowly—she is convinced that the desired end exists ideally, waiting to be achieved. It is because she does actually believe in progress that she can see, in the perspective of her view, this Covenant, and, later, more liberal covenants, as steps toward an ultimate goal.

THE EXCHANGE WITH SOVIET AMBASSADOR VISHINSKY

The clash between Eleanor Roosevelt and Andrei Vishinsky was considered by diplomats and journalists to be a highlight of the first United Nations sessions. It vividly illustrated the conflicting ideologies and worldviews of the U.S.-led Western Bloc and the Soviet-led Eastern Bloc. The so-called Cold War that raged between East and West for the next forty-five years had just begun. While ER tried until her death to prevent military conflict between the two camps, she did believe the Eastern assumptions should be challenged and engaged. The *New York Times* carried the following excerpts from the Roosevelt-Vishinsky exchange:

MRS. ROOSEVELT

I realize that the other delegates speak from different points of view and I understand why to them this seems different from what it does to me.

I cannot remember a political or a religious refugee being sent out of my country since the Civil War. At that time I do remember that one of my own relatives, because he came to this country and built a ship that ran contraband to the South, was not included in the amnesty. But since then this has not been a question that has entered into my thinking.

Europe has had a succession of wars and changes in population, as well as changes in ownership of land; and therefore it is natural that we approach the question from a different point of view; but we here in the United Nations are trying to frame things which will be broader in outlook, which will consider first the rights of man, which will consider what makes man more free: not governments but man.

I happen to come from the United States. I used in the committee an example; I am going to use it again; it is purely hypothetical. We happen to have an island in the Caribbean called Puerto Rico. Now in Puerto Rico there are several factions. One faction would like to become another State. Another faction would like to be entirely free. Another faction would like to stay just the way they are in their relation to the United States.

Suppose, just for the sake of supposing, that we had a refugee camp. We belong to the United Nations, but are we going to say that the Puerto Ricans, who happen to want to be free from the United States, shall receive no letter from home, none of their home papers, no letters perhaps from people who have gone to live in other places or information from other places? I think that we can stand up under having them free to get whatever information comes their way and make up their own minds. They are free human beings.

What is propaganda? Are we so weak in the United Nations, are we as individual nations so weak that we are going to forbid human beings to say what they think and fear whatever their friends and their particular type of mind happens to believe in? Surely we can tell them, their own Governments can tell them, all we want to tell them. We are not preventing them from hearing what each country wants them to hear, but we are saying, for instance, that in the United States we have people who have come there from war-torn Europe. They are in two different camps. They will write their relatives as they hear they are in different camps in Europe and they may not always say things that are exactly polite or in agreement with the United Nations. They may even say things against the United States, but I still think it is their right to say them and it is the right of men in refugee camps and women to hear them and to make their own decisions.

I object to "no propaganda against the United Nations or any member of the United Nations." It is like saying you are always sure you are going to be right. I am not always sure my Government or my nation will be right. I hope it will be and I shall do my best to keep it as right as I can keep it, and so, I am sure, will every other nation. But there are people who are going to disagree and I think we aim to reach a point where we on the whole are so right that the majority of our people will be with us and we can always stand having among us the people who do not agree, because we are sure that the right is so carefully guarded among us and the freedom of people is so carefully guarded that we will always have the majority with us.

For that reason I oppose including in a report which we have to accept this amendment, which I consider restrictive of human rights and human freedom.

MR. VISHINSKY

What was the thesis supported by Mrs. Roosevelt? Mrs. Roosevelt spoke in favor of unlimited freedom, and I think that this thesis is not correct. First, I think that such unlimited freedom does not exist and cannot exist in any country. I think, on the other hand, that it is indispensable to bring a limitation to the will and to the action of nations and peoples.

Can we admit unlimited freedom? I think it is impossible to admit such unlimited freedom. I think it is impossible to say that no conditions of limitation can ever be abstract. This does not take into account the real conditions of life. This cannot exist in present historical conditions.

Therefore, it is impossible not to limit the actions of man, and this action is limited by laws. Take criminal law first. Criminal law on the one hand allows to be done what is allowed and on the other hand limits the action of man, saying that man cannot do what is forbidden and cannot act against the interests of the law.

Thus the will of man is limited, limited by the will of other people, by the interest of all, and this is true also in the case of nations and of states. A state is not free to do all that it wants to do. A state is not free to be an aggressor. When a state becomes an aggressor democracy rises and democracy either diverts the state from its course of aggression or destroys the state. This happened to Hitler.

What is the question of principle which is involved here? The question of principle is that it is impossible to have unlimited freedom; it is impossible in the interests of society; it is impossible in the Organization of the United Nations. Freedom is limited by life itself.

The point is not a question of freedom of propaganda; we are not asking that freedom of speech or propaganda should be limited. What we are asking is that the incitement which leads to the commission of crime against the members of the United Nations should be limited. One cannot solve the problem without taking into account reality. The delegates for the United Kingdom and the United States have tried to solve this problem without regard to reality, and that is impossible. What is reality? Well, we see the camps with their thousands and tens of thousands of men whose souls and minds are corrupted and inflamed against their own countries: Yugoslavs who are provoked against Tito; Poles who are provoked against the Polish Government which has been recognized by the great powers.

It is against this propaganda that we speak, against this propaganda which is a crime because the incitement to a crime is itself a crime and in all countries there are laws which condemn and punish incitement to crime, incitement to crime being itself a crime.

The representative of the United Kingdom said that the words tolerance and pity may disappear from our vocabulary if we follow the way which our modest amendment invites us to follow. May I answer him by asking him whether in the past our tolerance was not too great and if we did not pay too much for this tolerance? The British people and other peoples, and above all the

Soviet people, paid too much for the past tolerance by which now some try to cloak the fascist propaganda. We do not want to accept tolerance. We paid too much for it; we paid too much in blood and we paid too much in life. One thousand seven hundred of our towns have been destroyed; tens of thousands of our villages have been destroyed, and millions and millions of men killed. Whole areas in our country are entirely desolate after the passage to and fro of Hitler's armies, and thank God, they were obliged to pass and to leave our country. We are afraid of a tolerance which gives such results. We do not want to accept such a tolerance.

It is easy to see in this exchange the reasons East and West had so much trouble for so many years living at peace with each other. Their assumptions about human nature, their visions of what the world in the future should be, even their definitions of words such as "freedom," "propaganda," "tolerance," and "law" were diametrically opposed. At center stage in Act I of this drama, ER helped clarify the debate, while emphasizing that it be confined to words, not military deeds.

A "NEW DEAL" FOR THE WORLD: ELEANOR ROOSEVELT AND THE ISSUE OF HUMAN RIGHTS

During the 1946 session, the United Nations General Assembly appointed a temporary Human Rights Commission. When it met in January 1947, Eleanor Roosevelt was elected its chair. The Commission considered several proposals for a universal declaration of human rights and recommended a permanent eighteen-member commission to frame such a document. The General Assembly ratified the recommendation, and President Truman appointed ER to be the United States representative. Now she had a chance to broaden the New Deal (her vision of the New Deal had always been more radical, reformist, and inclusive than FDR's) to include the world. It is not an exaggeration to say that she took the American mind, which she had helped create, to the world; she also brought the world, with all its problems and opportunities, to the American mind.

The Drafting of the United Nations Document on Human Rights

ER considered the United Nations Universal Declaration of Human Rights not only one of her own most lasting achievements but perhaps one of history's most important statements on the subject. In the following passage she describes the exciting but at times difficult process of creating the Declaration, which she considered her "most important task at the UN." She had a lot to learn about the economic and cultural nuances of international diplomacy—but learn she did.

After I had been elected chairman of the commission I tried to push our work along as rapidly as possible. I might point out here that eventually we decided that our main task was to write an International Bill of Rights. This was to consist of three parts. First, there was to be a Declaration, which would be adopted as a resolution of the General Assembly and would name and define all the human rights, not only the traditionally recognized political and civil rights but also the more recently recognized social, economic and cultural rights. Since the General Assembly is not a world parliament, its resolutions are not legally binding on member states. We therefore decided that the Declaration would be followed by a Covenant (or covenants) which would take the form of a treaty and would be legally binding on the countries that accepted them. Finally, there was to be a system for the implementation or enforcement of the rights.

We also finally recommended that the Human Rights Commission be composed of eighteen members, each of whom would represent one of the United Nations governments, and that they should be chosen on a rotating basis with due regard for geographical distribution, except for the representatives of the five great powers—the United States, Soviet Russia, the United Kingdom, France and China. As was customary, it was agreed that these five powers should be elected automatically to the new commission as members, leaving thirteen seats to be rotated among other members of the United Nations. These recommendations, however, came later. At the Hunter College sessions we were just getting started.

When we called for a formal vote on presenting our proposals to the Economic and Social Council, the Soviet Union merely recorded its "objections and dissent" to certain agreements and thus did not join in the recommendations of the preparatory commission. The Council accepted our recommendations and President Truman then nominated me as the United States representative on the commission. Being the first chairman of the commission, in addition to my duties as a delegate to the Assembly, kept me on United Nations work during five or six months of the year and I had to keep my daily schedule on a crowded timetable basis, with no minutes to spare.

* * *

In those days my life went long at that pace for long periods at a time and I suppose I enjoyed it, because I like to keep busy. When the United Nations headquarters was at Lake Success my schedule was complicated by the fact that I always had duties to attend to in New York early in the day and then had to drive for forty minutes to reach Lake Success in time for the opening of the Assembly or some other meeting at eleven o'clock. This suited Mr. Sandifer or any adviser because he always knew that I would be starting out at twenty minutes after ten. He could climb into my automobile with the assurance that for the next forty minutes I would be his "captive audience" and that our discussion of the day's work would not be interrupted.

In the period that I presided as chairman of the Human Rights Commission we spent most of our time trying to write the Universal Declaration of Human Rights and the Covenants, and there were times when I was getting in over my head. The officers of the commission had been charged with the task of preparing the first draft of the Declaration, and I remember that on one occasion, thinking that our work might be helped by an informal atmosphere, I asked this small group to meet at my apartment for tea. One of the members was the Chinese representative, Dr. P. C. Chang, who was a great joy to all of us because of his sense of humor, his philosophical observations, and his ability to quote some apt Chinese proverb to fit almost any occasion. Dr. John P. Humphrey, a Canadian who was the permanent head of the Division of Human Rights in the UN Secretariat, and Dr. Charles Malik of Lebanon, one of the very able diplomats at the United Nations, also were at this meeting.

As we settled down over the teacups, one of them made a remark with philosophic implications, and a heated discussion ensued. Dr. Chang was a pluralist and held forth in charming fashion on the proposition that there is more than one kind of ultimate reality. The Declaration, he said, should reflect more than Western ideas and Dr. Humphrey would have to be eclectic in his approach. His remark, though addressed to Dr. Humphrey, was really directed at Dr. Malik, from whom it drew a prompt retort as he expounded at length the philosophy of Thomas Aquinas. Dr. Humphrey joined enthusiastically in the discussion, and I remember that at one point Dr. Chang suggested that the Secretariat might well spend a few months studying the fundamentals of Confucianism! By that time I could not follow them, so lofty had the conversation become, so I simply filled the teacups again and sat back to be entertained by the talk of these learned gentlemen.

Early in the meetings of the commission we discovered that while it would be possible to reach some kind of agreement on the Declaration, we were going to be in for a great deal of controversy with the Russian representatives, particularly Dr. Pavlov, who attempted at every opportunity to write a bit of Communist philosophy into the document. For example, at the end of practically every article the Russian proposed to amend the Declaration to read: "This shall be enforced by the state."

When such an amendment was proposed I, or one of the other Western delegates, would argue against it on the ground that this was an international declaration by the United Nations and that we did not believe it should be imposed by the power of the individual governments. We would then ask for a vote and the amendment would be defeated. But as soon as the next article was completed the Soviet delegate would again propose the same amendment and we would have to go through the whole business again with the same result, the defeat of the Soviet proposal. This naturally became monotonous but the Russians never gave up trying.

The drafting of the articles continued over many months. During our early work on the Covenants and measures of implementation it became apparent that it was going to be exceedingly difficult to agree on articles that would, if accepted, be legally binding on the various nations. This was difficult enough in regard to civil and political rights that have become fairly well accepted throughout the civilized world, but when it came to economic and social rights it seemed to me at times that agreement would be all but impossible. These articles have, however, now been adopted by the majority of the committee.

The reason for this, in part at least, was the vast social and economic differences between the various countries; the social and economic conditions in the United States, for example, as contrasted to existing conditions in a country like India. The gap was so great that it was well-nigh impossible to phrase concepts acceptable to both countries. Let me give one example to explain these difficulties.

With the aid of various specialized United Nations agencies, we set out to write the best possible article aimed at the encouragement of universal education. We achieved a preliminary draft that stated that everyone had a right to primary, secondary and higher education, the first two to be compulsory but all of them eventually to be provided free by the individual governments concerned. This might read well to a citizen of the United States but it was quite a different matter in India.

"Our economy is strained," Madame Hansa Mehta, the Indian representative, explained, "and we are trying only to give all children a primary education. What would happen if we suddenly attempted to provide secondary and higher education, too? The article should be amended to read that the goal is to be accomplished gradually, with due consideration for the economy of each country."

"The trouble with that," I replied, "is that I do not believe the United States Senate would ever ratify a treaty so vaguely worded. The senators would ask: 'What does gradually mean—five years or ten years or a hundred years?' I just don't believe they would accept it."

But if the economic problems of underdeveloped countries provided one stumbling block, the political systems of other countries, particularly the United States, provided another. Our delegation had to insist on including a states' rights clause because we could act only in regard to matters that were under jurisdiction of the federal government. We had to explain that in other matters, which were under the control of the states, we had power only to "recommend" that the states take appropriate action. Australia and Canada were the only other countries in a similar position.

Many of the other countries resented the fact that they were being asked to commit all their people to the instruments we were drafting, whereas on certain matters the United States delegation could commit only a limited number of the people and hope that the various state governments would accept our recommendations. I could understand their resentment and their opposition to our "states' rights" system, but we always fought to get our amendment in. So far, however, the draft Covenants still lack a federal states' rights clause. We made slow progress in drafting the legally binding Covenants and even slower progress in framing measures of implementation that would provide means to enforce the Covenants.

Late in 1947 it was decided that the next meeting of the Human Rights Commission would be in Geneva, so we left for that city early in December with the idea of completing our work in time to be home for Christmas. As chairman, I knew that it would require much hard work and long hours to be able to adjourn before Christmas but I was in a determined mood and I warned all the delegations of my plans.

I immediately laid out a schedule of work that, with night sessions, I believed would enable us to adjourn by eleven o'clock on the evening of December 17.

Nobody objected to my plans, at least not until later, and I must say that everyone worked hard. My own day started at eight o'clock, when I met with my advisers at breakfast and went over the work schedule and any difficult problems. Then I would go to the Palais des Nations Unies, where the sessions were held and get through my correspondence in time for the morning session of the commission. At luncheon we usually got several delegates together to continue our discussions informally and then returned to the afternoon meeting. At night we had an after-dinner session or a meeting of our delegation. Later Mr. Hendrick and I would talk for perhaps an hour about the next day's plans, and after he had gone to bed Mrs. Hendrick would come in with a pile of personal letters on which we worked until after midnight. By the time I had dictated my daily newspaper column I was ready for bed.

This was a grueling schedule for everybody and within a few days I was being denounced—mostly in fun, I hope—as a merciless slave driver. But I must say we got through a great deal of work and kept to our schedule, for which I was very grateful to all the delegations.

We did end our work at eleven o'clock on the evening I had originally designated.

Our efforts to write a Charter or International Bill of Human Rights reached a kind of climax at the Paris sessions of the General Assembly in 1948. After our Geneva meeting we made steady progress on the Declaration, despite many controversies with the delegates from Communist countries.

Dr. Pavlov was a member of the commission and delivered many long propaganda harangues that appeared to be more for the purpose of publicizing the Communist point of view than in the hope of making changes in the Declaration. He was an orator of great power; his words rolled out of his black beard like a river, and stopping him was difficult. Usually, we had to sit and listen, but on one occasion it seemed to me that the rash accusations he brought against the United States and Great Britain were proving a real detriment to our work. Dr. Pavlov knew that most of us were getting tired of listening, but toward the end of one week when we were preparing to recess he began speaking again. He seemed likely to go on forever, but I watched him closely until he had to pause for breath. Then I banged the gavel so hard that the other delegates jumped in surprise and, before he could continue, I got in a few words of my own.

"We are here," I said, "to devise ways of safeguarding human rights. We are not here to attack each other's governments, and I hope when we return on Monday the delegate of the Soviet Union will remember that!" I banged the gavel again. "Meeting adjourned!"

Eventually we completed a draft of the Universal Declaration of Human Rights that we foolishly felt would be quickly accepted by the General Assembly, which was meeting in Paris in the autumn of 1948.

"I believe," General Marshall, who had become secretary of state, said before we left for Paris, "that this session of the General Assembly will be remembered as the human rights session."

As the session opened I was full of confidence that we could quickly get the Declaration through the formal hearings before Committee Three and have it approved by the Assembly. My confidence was soon gone. We worked for two months, often until late at night, debating every single word of that draft Declaration over and over again before Committee Three would approve its transmission to the General Assembly.

* * *

In the end there was no vote cast against the Declaration in the General Assembly, but there were some disappointing abstentions. The Soviet Union and its satellite countries abstained, since the Russian delegate contended that the Declaration put emphasis mainly on "eighteenth century rights" and not enough on economic, social and cultural rights. The delegate from Saudi Arabia abstained, saying he was quite sure King Ibn Saud would not agree to the interpretation of the Koran. South Africa also abstained, I was sad to note; its delegate said that they hoped to give their people basic human rights, but that the Declaration went too far. Two small countries were absent. The Declaration was finally accepted by the General Assembly on December 10, 1948.

After the Declaration was accepted, it seemed to me that the United States had held the chairmanship of the Commission on

Human Rights long enough. So at the 1951 meeting of the commission in Geneva, I nominated Charles Malik of Lebanon, with the consent of my government. He was elected and from then on I was just a member but a most interested member, for I believed the Human Rights Commission was one of the important parts of the foundation on which the United Nations might build a peaceful world.

The commission continued to work on drafting the Covenants, but this was so difficult that the United States group finally decided that it would be possible to progress only if we moved forward a step at a time. We proposed that there be two Covenants, one covering legally binding agreements on social and economic rights and another covering political and civil rights. This plan was vigorously opposed by some delegations, including the Soviets, on the ground that the economic and social rights were the most important and that they probably would not be accepted for years if they were in a separate covenant. But it seemed to our delegation that it was better to try to get what we could at that time. The civil and political rights already were a part of the law in many countries and were not so difficult to phrase in legal language that would be generally acceptable, although we knew that even this first step would be exceedingly difficult.

We finally won our point by only four votes, but taking the first step turned out to be even harder than we had expected. Progress had been made, but the Covenants were not well drafted, nor is the drafting yet complete, and I doubt whether they are likely to be accepted in their present form. Looking back over the work that has been done, I now believe it would be best to start anew by putting into the Covenant on civil and political rights only a few basic rights on which all could agree and to provide for adding other rights as it becomes possible to have them generally accepted.

In April 1948, as the Human Rights Commission drafted its declaration, ER wrote in the magazine *Foreign Affairs,* "The work of the Commission has been of outstanding value in setting before men's eyes the ideals which they must strive to reach. Men cannot live by bread alone." When the declaration passed late that year, she predicted that the General Assembly that met in Paris in 1948 would be known as the "Rights of Man Assembly." The document she worked so hard to have adopted, which follows, is a memorial to her ideals, her persistence, and her political skills. In the American vernacular, it has her name written all over it.

ER with Universal Declaration of Human Rights: "Engineer who built bridges over which all men could walk with dignity"

Universal Declaration of Human Rights

Passed by the United Nations General Assembly
December 10, 1948

(Text of the Declaration as passed and proclaimed by the General Assembly of the United Nations on Dec. 10, 1948)

WHEREAS recognition of the inherent dignity and of the equal and inalienable rights of all members of the human family is the foundation of freedom, justice and peace in the world,

WHEREAS disregard and contempt for human rights have resulted in barbarous acts which have outraged the conscience of mankind, and the advent of a world in which human beings shall enjoy freedom of speech and belief and freedom from fear and want has been proclaimed as the highest aspiration of the common people,

WHEREAS it is essential, if man is not to be compelled to have recourse, as a last resort, to rebellion against tyranny and oppression, that human rights should be protected by the rule of law,

WHEREAS it is essential to promote the development of friendly relations among nations,

WHEREAS the peoples of the United Nations have in the Charter reaffirmed their faith in fundamental human rights, in the dignity and worth of the human person and in the equal rights of men and women and have determined to promote social progress and better standards of life in larger freedom,

WHEREAS Member States have pledged themselves to achieve, in co-operation with the United Nations, the promotion of universal respect for and observance of human rights and fundamental freedoms,

WHEREAS a common understanding of these rights and freedoms is of the greatest importance, for the full realization of this pledge,

NOW THEREFORE THE GENERAL ASSEMBLY PROCLAIMS this Universal Declaration of Human Rights as a common standard of achievement for all peoples and all nations, to the end that every individual and every organ of society, keeping this Declaration constantly in mind, shall strive by teaching and education to promote respect for these rights and freedoms and by progressive measures, national and international, to secure their universal and effective recognition and observance, both among the peoples of Member States themselves and among the peoples of territories under their jurisdiction.

Article 1
All human beings are born free and equal in dignity and rights. They are endowed with reason and conscience and should act towards one another in a spirit of brotherhood.

Article 2
1—Everyone is entitled to all the rights and freedoms set forth in this Declaration, without distinction of any kind, such as race, color, sex, language, religion, political or other opinion, national or social origin, property, birth or other status.

2—Furthermore, no distinction shall be made on the basis of the political, jurisdictional or international status of the country or territory to which a person belongs, whether this territory be an independent, Trust, Non-Self-Governing territory, or under any other limitation of sovereignty.

Article 3
Everyone has the right to life, liberty and the security of person.

Article 4
No one shall be held in slavery or servitude; slavery and the slave trade shall be prohibited in all their forms.

Article 5
No one shall be subjected to torture or to cruel inhuman or degrading treatment or punishment.

Article 6
Everyone has the right to recognition everywhere as a person before the law.

Article 7
All are equal before the law and are entitled without any discrimination to equal protection of the law. All are entitled to equal protection against any discrimination in violation of this Declaration and against any incitement to such discrimination.

Article 8
Everyone has the right to an effective remedy by the competent national tribunals for acts violating the fundamental rights granted him by the constitution or by law.

Article 9
No one shall be subjected to arbitrary arrest, detention or exile.

Article 10
Everyone is entitled in full equality to a fair and public hearing by an independent and impartial tribunal, in the determination of his rights and obligations and of any criminal charge against him.

Article 11
1—Everyone charged with a penal offence has the right to be presumed innocent until proved guilty according to law in a public trial at which he has had all the guarantees necessary for his defence.

2—No one shall be held guilty of any penal offence on account of any act or omission which did not constitute a penal offence, under national or international law, at the time when it was committed. Nor shall a heavier penalty be imposed than the one that was applicable at the time the penal offence was committed.

Article 12
No one shall be subjected to arbitrary interference with his privacy, family, home or correspondence, to attacks upon his honor and reputation. Everyone has the right to the protection of the law against such interference or attacks.

Article 13
1—Everyone has the right to freedom of move and residence within the borders of each state.

2—Everyone has the right to leave any country, including his own, and to return to his country.

Article 14

1—Everyone has the right to seek and to enjoy in other countries asylum from persecution.

2—This right may not be invoked in the case prosecutions genuinely arising from non-politic crimes or from acts contrary to the purposes and principles of the United Nations.

Article 15

1—Everyone has the right to a nationality.

2—No one shall be arbitrarily deprived of his nationality nor denied the right to change his nationality.

Article 16

1—Men and women of full age, without any limitation due to race, nationality or religion, have the right to marry and to found a family. They are entitled to equal rights as to marriage, during marriage and at its dissolution.

2—Marriage shall be entered into only with the free and full consent of the intending spouses.

3—The family is the natural and fundamental group unit of society and is entitled to protection by society and the State.

Article 17

1—Everyone has the right to own property alone as well as in association with others.

2—No one shall be arbitrarily deprived of his property.

Article 18

Everyone has the right to freedom of thought, conscience and religion; this right includes freedom to change his religion or belief, and freedom, either alone or in community with others and in public or private, to manifest his religion or belief in teaching, practice, worship and observance.

Article 19

Everyone has the right to freedom of opinion and expression; this right includes freedom to hold opinions without interference and to seek, receive and impart information and ideas through any media and regardless of frontiers.

Article 20

1—Everyone has the right to freedom of peaceful assembly and association.

2—No one may be compelled to belong to an association.

Article 21

1—Everyone has the right to take part in the government of his country, directly or through freely chosen representatives.

2—Everyone has the right of equal access to public service in his country.

3—The will of the people shall be the basis of the authority of government; this will shall be expressed in periodic and genuine elections which shall be by universal and equal suffrage and shall be held by secret vote or by equivalent free voting procedures.

Article 22

Everyone, as a member of society, has the right to social security and is entitled to relations through national effort and international co-operation and in accordance with the organization and resources of each State, of the economic, social and cultural rights indispensable for his dignity and the free development of his personality.

Article 23

1—Everyone has the right to work, to free choice of employment, to just and favorable conditions of work and to protection against unemployment.

2—Everyone, without any discrimination, has the right to equal pay for equal work.

3—Everyone who works has the right to just and favorable remuneration insuring for himself and his family an existence worthy of human dignity, and supplemented, if necessary, by other means of social protection.

4—Everyone has the right to form and to join trade unions for the protection of his interests.

Article 24

Everyone has the right to rest and leisure, including reasonable limitation of working hours and periodic holidays with pay.

Article 25

1—Everyone has the right to a standard of living adequate for the health and well-being of himself and of his family, including food, clothing, housing and medical care and necessary social services, and the right to security in the event of unemployment, sickness, disability, widowhood, old age or other lack of livelihood in circumstances beyond his control.

2—Motherhood and childhood are entitled to special care and assistance. All children, whether born in or out of wedlock, shall enjoy the same social protection.

Article 26

1—Everyone has the right to education. Education shall be free, at least in the elementary and fundamental stages. Elementary education shall be compulsory. Technical and professional education shall be made generally available and higher education shall be equally accessible to all on the basis of merit.

2—Education shall be directed to the full development of the human personality and to the strengthening of respect for human rights and fundamental freedoms. It shall promote understanding, tolerance and friendship among all nations, racial or religious groups, and shall further the activities of the United Nations for the maintenance of peace.

3—Parents have a prior right to choose the kind of education that shall be given to their children.

Article 27

1—Everyone has the right freely to participate in the cultural life of the community, to enjoy the arts and, to share in scientific advancement and its benefits.

2—Everyone has the right to the protection of the moral and material interests resulting from any scientific, literary or artistic production of which he is the author.

Article 28

Everyone is entitled to a social and international order in which the rights and freedoms set forth in this Declaration can be fully realized.

Article 29

1—Everyone has duties to the community in which alone the free and full development of his personality is possible.

2—In the exercise of his rights and freedoms, everyone shall be subject only to such limitations as are determined by law solely for the purpose of due recognition and respect for the rights and freedoms of others and of meeting the just requirements of morality, public order and the general welfare in a democratic society.

3—These rights and freedoms may in no case be exercised contrary to the purposes and principles of the United Nations.

Article 30

Nothing in this Declaration may be interpreted implying for any State, group or person any right to engage in any activity or to perform any act aimed at the destruction of any of the rights and freedoms set forth herein.

ER went to great lengths to draft, pass, and encourage the enforcement of human rights around the world. She gave talks on the Voice of America radio network, similar to the "fireside chats" FDR had given the American people during his presidency; and she spoke equally well in English, Spanish, French, Italian, and German. She served as a United States representative to the United Nations until she was pointedly not reappointed by the new Republican President, Dwight D. Eisenhower, when he took office in 1953. Then she joined the American Association for the United Nations and continued to speak out in support of what she considered "the one organization that has the machinery to bring together all the nations in an effort to maintain world peace." She spoke as much to Americans as to the peoples of other nations. She wanted to make the ideals of the UN part of the American mind. Her ideals, the ideals of the United Nations, the ideals of the Universal Declaration are only in the beginning stages of being fully accepted around the world, but ER takes her full share of credit for that beginning. In 1958 she returned to address the UN General Assembly. At that occasion she recalled her days working on the Human Rights Declaration and concluded:

> Where, after all, do universal human rights begin? In small places, close to home—so close and so small they cannot be seen on any maps of the world. Yet they are the world of the individual person; the neighborhood he lives in; the school or college he attends; the factory, farm or office where he works. Such are the places where every man, woman and child seeks equal justice, equal opportunity, equal dignity without discrimination. Unless these rights have meaning there, they have little meaning anywhere. Without concerned citizen action to uphold them close to home, we shall look in vain for progress in the larger world.

AN ASSESSMENT OF ELEANOR ROOSEVELT'S WORK AT THE UNITED NATIONS, BY COLLEEN O'CONNOR

Colleen O'Connor, a historian who has written extensively on women's issues, has studied ER's years at the United Nations between 1946 and 1952. The following excerpt is from a chapter she contributed to the book *Eleanor Roosevelt: An American Journey*. Note O'Connor's emphasis on the roles ER's aristocratic bearing, her "star quality" as a former First Lady, and her female gender played in her success at the United Nations.

Eleanor Roosevelt's tenure at the United Nations was, in her estimation, one of the "most wonderful and worthwhile experiences" of her life. It was also one of the most telling. This part of her public life, perhaps more than any other, reflects the activities of a mature, independent woman at her most serene and an accomplished politician at her most earnest. The private cost of such public dedication was considerable.

Eleanor Roosevelt believed in the United Nations and expended her considerable personal and diplomatic skills to make it work. She also pursued her own time-honored agenda for success—accept a challenge, prove yourself, speak from conviction, pave the way for other women of like-minded persuasions and never be rude. Roosevelt adhered to each of these tenets during her UN years.

This combination of discipline and dedication, subtle as it may have seemed, was understood by people as far removed from the political arena as movie director John Huston. He summed it up best when directing Katharine Hepburn in the film *African Queen,* being shot on location in the Belgian Congo. Hepburn had difficulty portraying the personality of Rose Sayer, a dignified, independent-minded churchmarm who joined Humphrey Bogart on his ramshackled boat for a World War I escape down the river.

"Play her," Huston told the troubled Hepburn, "like Eleanor Roosevelt"—fiercely determined, self-contained and ultimately quite courageous. Hepburn did and just missed beating out Vivien Leigh for an Oscar.

At least one observer felt that the implications of Hepburn playing Rose like Eleanor Roosevelt had repercussions far beyond that one movie. "Something of the notion of Hepburn as Roosevelt, of Hepburn as American royalty . . . stayed in the public's mind," he believed. Indeed, the notion of Eleanor Roosevelt as the original model for American royalty grew in large part from her work at the United Nations.

Despite her considerable political experience, Eleanor Roosevelt approached her UN job in fear. As the proud bearer of the Roosevelt name and tradition, she knew a great deal would be expected of her. She, who was the wife of a former president of the United States, the niece of another president, the mother of six children, and by her estimates the hostess in one year to "over four thousand for lunch, more than nine thousand for tea, and others for dinner almost every night when [she] was not traveling," doubted her ability to represent her country in this new international forum. When first asked by Truman to be a US representative, her reaction was, "How could I be a delegate to help

organize the United Nations when I have no background or experience in international meetings?" How, she also wondered,
would she measure up against some of the best negotiators the
international community could spare—the Russians' A. P. Pavlov,
the French Rene Cassin, India's Jawaharlal Nehru—or some of the
best thinkers, such as Confucian scholar Dr. Peng-Chung Chang;
the Lebanese Christian student of Thomas Aquinas, Dr. Charles H.
Malik; or even the more troubling political members of her own
delegation who disapproved of her nomination—Senator Arthur
Vandenburg and John Foster Dulles?

She recognized that Truman's offer was made, in part, to
strengthen his own political popularity and support, but accepted
the invitation because she believed the UN "to be the one hope
for a peaceful world." Throughout her professional diplomatic
career she struggled to lend her prestige and influence to that
young deliberative body in order that it might better succeed.
She faced powerful foes in realizing that hope.

Once she accepted the nomination, Roosevelt decided, as
always, to be herself and to remember the words of her husband's
political adviser, Louis Howe: "Don't show yourself as a know-it-
all," he told her, "appear stupid. Then when you do vouchsafe
some information or knowledge everyone will say 'how brilliant!'"

When Eleanor Roosevelt approached the gangplank of the
Queen Elizabeth for her transatlantic voyage to London and her
first UN meeting, she was seized by wonder, fear and exhilaration.
As she confessed to one reporter on the ship, "For the first time in
my life I can say just what I want. For your information it is wonderful to feel free." Not only was she without Franklin, without
her devoted secretary, "Tommy," and without an entourage; she
was also happily without the burdens and constraints of being
First Lady. She could think for herself not only in private, but,
within State Department limits, in public as well. The new United
Nations provided Eleanor Roosevelt with the first real public challenge she could call her own. Except for a stormy, four month job
as associate director of the Office of Civil Defense in 1941–1942,
Eleanor Roosevelt had never held an independent government
position. She feared failure, not only for herself but for those
women who might wish to follow her in other diplomatic posts.
She refused to countenance defeat.

* * *

Having both accepted the challenge and proved herself in
the first session in London, Eleanor Roosevelt turned to the next
goal—including like-minded women in politics. She pushed for

the nomination of Helen Gahagan Douglas, first-term congress-woman from California, to the second session of the UN.

Douglas and Roosevelt had met in the late thirties. Roosevelt, the mentor, encouraged Douglas, wife of actor Melvyn Douglas and herself a former actress and opera singer, to become active in Democratic politics. At Eleanor's urging Helen worked herself up through the ranks of California party politics to head the women's division in the state and eventually become the hand-picked successor to the outgoing congressman and New Deal ally, Thomas Ford.

By the time of her election to the House in 1944, Douglas had already been a frequent and welcomed guest at the Roosevelt White House. Her appointment to the United Nations two years later as an alternate delegate (during her freshman term), and her congressional appointment to the prestigious House Foreign Affairs Committee, can be directly traced to the Roosevelt connection. She became such a trusted ally that when Eleanor wanted a job for Lorena Hickock, Douglas gave her one as her secretary at the UN.

Aside from obvious differences between the two women (Douglas was younger, extraordinarily beautiful and effusive, while Eleanor was not) there existed striking similarities. Both were raised in privileged backgrounds; both thought social graces mattered and that rudeness was abhorrent; both devoured their work, knew how to generate press and popular support for certain issues and appeared dauntless and indefatigable to all their friends.

Both Roosevelt and Douglas found the question of nuclear weapons to be a paramount issue and a critical factor in lending their support to the UN. In her first press conference after leaving the White House, Mrs. Roosevelt tried to explain her commitment to the United Nations:

> I think if the atomic bomb did nothing more, it scared the people to the point where they realized that either they must do something about preventing war or there is a chance that there might be a morning when we would not wake up.

The like-minded Douglas believed the lack of international control over nuclear weapons would result in "a scientific race for destruction," and would culminate in an all-consuming "holocaust." As she told her colleagues in the House of Representatives, "The real problem confronting us today is not the control of the atomic bomb for after the atomic bomb it may well be bacteriological warfare or some other new weapons which uncontrolled may destroy the world." She went on to quote Albert Einstein's message to her: "The release of atomic energy has not created a new problem. It has simply made more urgent the necessity of solving the existing ones."

At the UN these two women moved as of one mind. Perhaps one reason was the scarcity of other women. Of approximately 1,600 delegates, only seven were women. The countries who joined the United States in sending women were the Dominican Republic, Chile, Denmark, France and India. The former British colony took honors by naming Mrs. Vijaslakshmi Pandit, sister of Jawaharlal Nehru, head of their delegation. She, too, became a close friend of Eleanor Roosevelt's.

After leading the debate against apartheid in South Africa, the triumphant Mrs. Pandit left the chambers to sustained applause. Douglas, in perfect agreement with India's position against racism, waited for her in the members' anteroom. As a friend remembered:

> Mrs. Pandit came into the lounge and Helen grabbed her and instead of bending to kiss her, she took her sort of by the elbows and just lifted her up and kissed her. And there were great cheers in the lounge.

Not all took the women delegates' presence seriously. The *Baltimore Sun* struck the prevalent glamour-girl theme of the forties when reporting on Douglas. As the paper informed its readers:

> The tall, good-looking brunette with upswept hair is President Truman's gift to the United Nation's [*sic*] Assembly.
> She's Helen Gahagan Douglas, 45 and as fabulous as they come —from California.

The cost to both Douglas and Roosevelt for leading high-profile public lives included a great deal of hostility. They were publicly criticized for stretching the acceptable parameters of women's roles, for being too liberal, and for their close friendship.

Mrs. Roosevelt was reappointed as a delegate to the next session of the UN but Douglas served only one term. She failed to earn reappointment because she angered Truman with her New Deal loyalties and by her outspoken criticism of his Cold War assumptions. Eleanor lamented her departure, writing to her, "I miss having you in the delegation." Mrs. Roosevelt continued to insist on the appointment of other women to the American delegation and was successful. Among those who served with her was Edith Sampson, a black lawyer.

* * *

The respect that Roosevelt had earned during her tenure in the United Nations was made evident during the General Assembly in 1948 when, after she delivered a speech, the other members responded with a standing ovation—the only delegate ever to be so honored.

Later during that same session, her most "important task," the Universal Declaration of Human Rights, passed without dissent and only eight abstentions. She wrote in her journal that night, "long job finished." Secretary General U Thant called the declaration "the Magna Carta of Mankind." An editorial in the *New York Times* hailed its passage as "Eleanor Roosevelt's victory." It is certainly— and rightfully—Eleanor Roosevelt's greatest legacy.

For her work on the Declaration of Human Rights, Eleanor Roosevelt was nominated for the Nobel Peace Prize three times. Adlai Stevenson, then U.S. representative to the United Nations, nominated her first in 1961. He nominated her again in 1962, with President John F. Kennedy seconding the nomination. Six months later, Eleanor Roosevelt died. In the summer of 1964 yet another effort to secure her the prize began, but was snagged on the Nobel Charter's provision that the award not be given post-humously. About this the ever-blunt Harry Truman wrote the Prize Committee:

> I understand that there are regulations in your committee that rule out an award of the Peace Prize to Mrs. Franklin D. Roosevelt because she has passed away. The award without the financial prize that goes with it can be made. You should make it. If she didn't earn it, then no one else did.

QUESTIONS FOR RESPONSIVE ESSAYS

1. How did Eleanor Roosevelt's experiences during the Great Depression and her work for New Deal legislation and programs, including the "networking" she did with other women, prepare her for her work at the United Nations? How did they help formulate her agenda and her strategy for attacking international problems?

2. How did ER overcome the objections and reservations of critics who opposed her nomination to the U.S. delegation to the United Nations? How did she use the place assigned her by skeptics to make herself the most celebrated person in that first delegation?

3. What does her exchange with Vishinsky say about her world philosophy and the spirit with which she explained it? What does it also tell us about future negotiations in the United Nations between the United States and the Soviet Union? To what extent did ER help both create and soften the rhetoric of the coming Cold War?

4. What was ER's role in drafting and passing the Universal Declaration of Human Rights at the United Nations? How realistic are its ideals and goals? How well have the nations of the world done in trying to achieve the goals of this document?

5. Analyze the Universal Declaration of Human Rights. Where do you see the hand of Eleanor Roosevelt? How does it reflect the ideals of her liberal, democratic philosophy? Has it been an effective tool to accomplish its ideals? How might it be circumvented by those who do not honor it?

PART IV

A First-Rate Conscience

Life was meant to be lived, and curiosity must be kept alive. One must never, for whatever reason, turn his back on life.

—ELEANOR ROOSEVELT
Autobiography, 1961

The First Lady's mountainous correspondence receives her personal attention, and she replies with an air of intimacy to each and every writer, her comments reflecting her own large experience in household and public affairs.

—MARY BEARD
Review of *It's Up to the Women*, 1933

The author Geoffrey Ward titled his biography of Franklin Roosevelt *A First Rate Temperament*. FDR's temperament, much more than his mind, made him the leader he was, the optimistic President who approached the Great Depression and World War II with confidence and who left such a legacy of hope. The same may be said of Eleanor Roosevelt's conscience, or, as we might have said in an earlier day, her heart. Much more than her mind, it was her conscience, her deep awareness of human need and her desire to remedy human suffering, that gave her the courage to tackle tough problems and to leave her legacy of compassion.

ER was almost fifty years old when she became First Lady. In that office, as we have learned, she served as FDR's eyes and ears and legs, just as she had done for twelve years before his election to the presidency. Upon becoming First Lady, however, she began to be more—more for him, more for herself. She had for years made speeches for him, teaching herself rhetorical skills she found hard to master; and in 1932 she began teaching herself to write, another skill that did not come easily to her, in order to reach a larger audience with his and her message of reform. She wrote books, articles for newspapers and magazines, a column called "My Day" that was syndicated to hundreds of newspapers from 1935 to 1960, and even an advice column that answered questions her readers sent to her. The books she wrote with deliberation, reflecting on what she wanted to say, choosing her phrases and sentences carefully. The columns and even the essays for the popular press she wrote quickly, dashing them off between appointments, sometimes dictating them to a secretary while "on the run." But all of her published work reflects her desire to reach a national audience, to test the acceptability of her liberal ideals, to share her liberal conscience, to press her agenda for social reform.

THE "MORAL BASIS" OF ELEANOR ROOSEVELT'S PHILOSOPHY

We begin this survey of ER's writings with a selection from her book, *The Moral Basis of Democracy*, published in 1940. Note that she addresses her thoughts primarily to young Americans, with whom she had cooperated to push for New Deal legislation and with whom she agonized over America's proper response to the war that in 1940 seemed inevitable. In this book she tells them that, despite daunting challenges, democracy will triumph. Here she reminds them that in order to triumph, it must stand on solid moral ground:

> In Jefferson's beliefs we get the clearest statements for his day of a true understanding of human beings. He wanted no slaves because he realized that slavery was the denial of the equality of man. It meant that if we denied equality to any man we lost the basis of Democracy. If we are honest with ourselves today, we will acknowledge that the ideal of Democracy has never failed, but that we haven't carried it out, and in our lack of faith we have debased the human being who must have a chance to live if Democracy is to be successful.
>
>   The slave is still with us, but his color is not always black, and I think we will also have to acknowledge that most of our difficulties

arise today from the fact that in the rush of material development we have neglected to keep close enough to the Revolutionary idea, guided by religious feeling, which is the basis of Democracy. We have undertaken, under our form of government, to carry out the ideal which can exist only if we accept the brotherhood of man as a basic truth in human society.

We may belong to any religion or to none, but we must acknowledge that the life of Christ was based on principles which are necessary to the development of a Democratic state. We accept that fact and measure every undertaking by that rule. But, it is easy to understand where our difficulties lie today. Even Thomas Paine[1] said: "The rights of property being inviolate and sacred, no one ought to be deprived of it, except in cases of evident public necessity, legally ascertained and on condition of a previous indemnity."

Our present situation, our present difficulties arise from the fact that in the development of civilization we have neglected to remember that the rights of all people to some property are inviolate. We have allowed a situation to arise where many people are debased by poverty or the accident of race, in our own country, and therefore have no stake in Democracy; while others appeal to this old rule of the sacredness of property rights to retain in the hands of a limited number the fruits of the labor of many.

We have never been willing to face this problem, to line it up with the basic, underlying beliefs in Democracy and to set our actions side by side with the actual example of the Christ-like way of living.

Thus, within our nation there are many who do not understand the values of Democracy, and we have been unable to spread these values throughout the world, because as a people we have been led by the gods of Mammon from the spiritual concepts and from the practical carrying-out of those concepts conceived for our nation as a truly free and democratic people.

* * *

We are, of course, going through a type of revolution and we are succeeding in bringing about a greater sense of social responsibility in the people as a whole. Through the recognition by our government of a responsibility for social conditions much has been accomplished; but there is still much to be done before we are

---

[1] Author of *Common Sense*, published in 1776. He helped spark the American War for Independence.

even prepared to accept some of the fundamental facts which will make it possible to fight as a unified nation against the new philosophies arrayed in opposition to Democracy.

It would seem clear that in a Democracy a minimum standard of security must at least be possible for every child in order to achieve the equality of opportunity which is one of the basic principles set forth as a fundamental of Democracy. This means achieving an economic level below which no one is permitted to fall, and keeping a fairly stable balance between that level and the cost of living. No one as yet seems to know just how to do this without an amount of planning which will be considered too restrictive for freedom. The line between domination and voluntary acquiescence in certain controls is a very difficult one to establish. Yet it is essential in a Democracy.

For a number of years we seemed to be progressing toward a condition in which war as a method of settling international difficulties might be eliminated, but with the rise of an opposing philosophy of force, this has become one of our main problems today. It brings before us the question of whether under the Democratic theory we can be efficient enough to meet the growing force of totalitarianism with its efficient organization for aggression.

This question is of special interest to youth, and added to the question of unemployment, it creates for them the main problem of existence.

The youth which is coming of age in our country today is living under a government which is attempting to meet a great many internal problems in new ways, and with methods never before tried. These ways are questioned by a great many people; but few people question the fact that the problems are with us and must be faced.

Youth seems to be more conscious than anyone else of the restrictions of opportunity which have come with our form of civilization. Some of these restrictions may be due to the development of the nation to a degree which leaves few physical frontiers to master; some of them may be due to a lack of social development, to a system which hasn't kept pace with the machine and made it possible to use advantageously more leisure time. Such malfunctioning makes it impossible to lessen the burden of labor without curtailing the volume of work, so that many people are left with nothing to do, and therefore without the wherewithal for living.

Nowhere in the world today has government solved these questions. Therefore, as their elders leave the stage, it remains for youth to find a way to face the domestic situation, to meet the conditions which confront their country in its relationship with the other countries of the world.

It is not enough to adopt the philosophies and methods which have appeared in other countries. These difficulties have been met elsewhere by deciding that one man who orders the lives of great numbers of people can best arrange for the equable distribution of the necessities of life. From the point of view of our Democratic philosophy and our relief in the welfare of the individual this has fatal drawbacks.

Youth must make a decision. It will have to decide whether religion, the spirit of social co-operation, is necessary to the development of a Democratic form of government and to the relationship which human beings must develop if they are to live happily together. If it is, youth will have to devise some means of bringing it more closely to the hearts and to the daily lives of everyone.

It is not entirely the fault of any of the churches, or of any of the various religious denominations that so many people, who call themselves Catholic, Protestant or Jew, behave as though religion were something shut up in one compartment of their lives. It seems to have no effect on their actions or their growth or on their relationship to their surroundings and activities. Leaders of religious thought have tried for generations to make us understand that religion is a way of life which develops the spirit. Perhaps, because of the circumstances which face us today, the youth of this generation may make this type of religion a reality, I think they might thus develop for the future of this country and of the world a conception of success which will change our whole attitude toward life and civilization.

* * *

There are two questions which young people in our country have to face. What are we prepared to sacrifice in order to retain the Democratic form of government?

What do we gain if we retain this form of government?

Let us consider first the sacrifices that we make in a real Democracy. Our basic sacrifice is the privilege of thinking and working for ourselves alone. From time immemorial the attitude of the individual has been one of selfishness. As civilization has advanced people have thought of their families, and finally of a group of people like themselves; but down in our hearts it has always been the interest which you and I had in ourselves primarily which has motivated us.

If we are able to have genuine Democracy we are going to think primarily of the rights and privileges and the good that may come to the people of a great nation. This does not mean, of course, that we are going to find everyone in agreement with us in what we think is for the good of the majority of the people; but it does mean that we will be willing to submit our ideas to the test of what the majority wishes.

That is a big sacrifice for Democracy. It means that we no longer hold the fruits of our labors as our own, but consider them in the light of a trusteeship. Just as the labor itself must be put into avenues which may no longer be bringing us what at one time we considered as satisfactory returns, but which are serving some socially useful purpose in the community in which we live. This does not mean that we will work any less hard. It does not mean that we will use less initiative or put less preparation into the field of work in which we are entering. It does mean, however, that we will execute to the best of our ability every piece of work which we undertake and give our efforts to such things as seem to us to serve the purposes of the greatest number of people.

The second sacrifice which we make for Democracy is to give to our government an interested and intelligent participation. For instance, if a city, town or county meeting is called, we will not find something more interesting or attractive to do that evening. We will go to the meeting, take part in it and try to understand what the questions and issues are. Thus we start the machinery of Democracy working from the lowest rung upward.

We often make the mistake of believing that what happens at the bottom makes no difference. As a matter of fact, it is what we do at the bottom which decides what eventually happens at the top. If all the way down the line every able-bodied citizen attended to his duties, went to the community meetings, tried to find out about the people who were going to hold office, knew the questions that came before them, there would be a radical change in the quality of people who take active part in political work.

We must have party machinery because there must be people who attend to such things as calling meetings, sending out notices, going from door to door to distribute literature or bring the issues to the voters before Election Day. These issues can be presented in many different ways, according to the understanding and the feeling of the people who present them. It would not be so difficult to find people to run for office if we knew that the citizens as a whole were going to know something about them and their ideas, and were going to vote not on a traditional basis, but according to their actual knowledge of the questions at stake and the personalities of the candidates. There would be less opportunity for calumny, for unfairness, and for the acceptance of untrue statements if, every step of the way, each individual took his responsibility seriously and actually did his job as a citizen in a Democracy.

There is no reward for this kind of citizenship except the reward of feeling that we really have a government which in every way represents the best thought of all the citizens involved. In such a Democracy a man will hold office not because it brings certain honors and considerations from his constituents, but because he has an obligation to perform a service to Democracy.

Perhaps the greatest sacrifice of all is the necessity which Democracy imposes on every individual to make himself decide in what he believes. If we believe in Democracy and that it is based on the possibility of a Christ-like way of life, then everybody must force himself to think through his own basic philosophy, his own willingness to live up to it and to help carry it out in everyday living.

The great majority of people accept religious dogmas handed to them by their parents without very much feeling of leaving a personal obligation to clarify their creed for themselves. But, if from our religion, whatever it may be, we are impelled to work out a way of life which leads to the support of a Democratic form of government, then we have a problem we cannot escape: we must know what we believe in, how we intend to live, and what we are doing for our neighbors.

Our neighbors, of course, do not include only the people whom we know; they include, also, all those who live anywhere within the range of our knowledge. That means an obligation to the coal miners and share-croppers, the migratory workers, to the tenement-house dwellers and the farmers who cannot make a living. It opens endless vistas of work to acquire knowledge and, when we have acquired it in our own country, there is still the rest of the world to study before we know what our course of action should be.

Again a sacrifice in time and thought, but a factor in a truly Democratic way of life.

Few members of the older generations have even attempted to make of themselves the kind of people who are really worthy of the power which is vested in the individual in a Democracy. We must fulfill our duties as citizens, see that our nation is truly represented by its government, see that the government is responsive to the will and desires of the people. We must make that will and desire of the people the result of adequate education and adequate material security. We must maintain a standard of living which makes it possible for the people really to want justice for all, rather than to harbor a secret hope for privileges because they cannot hope for justice.

If we accomplish this, we have paved the way for the first hope for real peace the world has ever known. All people desire peace, but they are led to war because what is offered them in this world seems to be unjust, and they are constantly seeking a way to right that injustice.

These are the sacrifices future generations will be called upon to make for a permanent Democracy which has a background of spiritual belief.

* * *

And now, what do we gain from Democracy?

The greatest gain, perhaps, is a sense of brotherhood, a sense that we strive together toward a common objective.

I have sat with groups of people who for a few short minutes were united by the ideas and aspirations that had been presented to them by leaders able to express their vision or their dreams.

Those few minutes have made clear to me the possibility of strength that some day might lie in a moral feeling of unity brought about by a true sense of brotherhood.

By achieving improvement in our own small sphere, we would gain, too, a tremendous satisfaction in realizing that we were actively participating in whatever happens in the world as a whole. The decisions at the top would be ours, because, in the first place, we had started choosing our men at the bottom and had thus brought about a real representation at the top. The new world which we conceived could become a reality, for these men, the leaders, would share the vision of the people.

It would be no Utopia, for the gains made by Democracy, which are the gains made by human beings over themselves, are never static. We fight for them and have to keep on fighting. The gains are slow and won in day by day effort. There is no chance for boredom or indifference because of a lack of further heights to climb. In such a society the heights are always before one, and the dread of slipping backward ever present.

One of the gains of Democracy would be that constant sense of vigilance and alertness which makes of life an adventure and gives it a continuous appeal. We cannot remove sorrow and disappointment from the lives of human beings, but we can give them an opportunity to free themselves from mass restrictions made by man.

There is nothing more exciting in the world than to be conscious of inwardly achieving something new; and anyone who puts into practice the life of Christ on earth, cannot fail to feel the growth in his own mastery over self. Under the Democracy based on such a religious impulse, there would still, of course, be leaders, and there would still be people of initiative interested and prodding other people to attempt the development of new ideas, or to participate in new enjoyments which they had not before understood or experienced.

Under such a Democracy the living standard of all the people would be gradually rising. That is what the youth of the next generation will be primarily interested in achieving, because that is the vital gain in Democracy for the future, if we base it on the Christian way of life as lived by Christ.

Early in her White House years ER began writing for the popular press, accepting pay for her articles and columns (which led to criticism from her detractors), contributing what she earned to charities (which she did not reveal). Her articles, which were in the form of essays, and her advice columns appeared in such journals as *New Republic, Look, Harper's,* and *Ladies Home Journal.* Her advice columns appeared both in newspapers and in *Ladies Home Journal, Woman's Home Companion,* and *McCall's.* Her opinions were considered by many people, both friend and foes, as "liberal." She was proud of the label because as she once wrote, "a liberal tries to see a question from as many points of view as possible and then decides which is the point of view which will benefit the greatest number of people."

These popular writings may be sorted into the responses she made to three categories of questions, those regarding public policy, those dealing with the personal problems of her readers, and those concerning questions of her private life.

HER OPINIONS ON PUBLIC MATTERS

While ER was not an elected official, she lived half of her life at the center of public affairs; and she knew them all from every angle, inside and outside. Thus her opinions, whether expressed in essays or in advice columns, were both informed and influential. The following are examples of her interest in and desire to solve certain problems.

An Essay on Racism

ER was always disturbed by the racism so prevalent in her supposedly democratic and egalitarian America. Slaves had been freed for nearly a century, yet black Americans were still subjected to lynchings and many forms of discrimination. She tried every way possible to get an anti-lynching law passed. She spoke out against segregation and discrimination at every opportunity, so often in fact that racists started the rumor that she was "part black." She met with black leaders and gave them every encouragement, even when it led to condemnation from members of her own Democratic Party in the South. In 1936 she invited black contralto Marian Anderson to sing at the White House; and in 1939 when the Daughters of the American Revolution refused to let Ms. Anderson sing at their Constitution Hall, she resigned her membership in the DAR and joined the National Association for the Advancement of Colored People.

World War II, when the United States allied itself against Japan, made her aware of racism in a broader context. For most of the twentieth century Chinese in America had been treated with hostility and segregated from whites in schools. Japanese in America were suspected of treasonous sympathy with the nation of their origin, a nation that on December 7, 1941, bombed Pearl Harbor in the Hawaiian Islands and provoked war.

When the following article appeared in the *New Republic* on May 11, 1942, the American government was about to round up all Japanese Americans in California and relocate them in what amounted to concentration camps for the duration of the war. The article's sentiments were daring at the time. Madame Chiang Kai-shek, whose articles on racism led ER to write the piece, was the influential wife of China's wartime leader.

ER here used the term "Negro" for a black American. This term was commonly used both by black and white Americans until the late 1960s, when "black" became the preferred designation. Today the term "African American" is also used.

"RACE, RELIGION AND PREJUDICE"

Madame Chiang-Kai Shek's recent articles force us all to realize that one of the phases of this war which we have to face is the question of race discrimination.

We have had a definite policy toward the Chinese and Japanese who wished to enter our country for many years, and I doubt very much if after this war is over we can differentiate among the peoples of Europe, the Near East and the Far East.

Perhaps the simplest way of facing the problem in the future is to say that we are fighting for freedom, and that one of the freedoms we must establish is freedom from discrimination among the peoples of the world, either because of race, or of color, or of religion.

The people of the world have suddenly begun to stir and they seem to feel that in the future we should look upon each other as fellow human beings, judged by our acts, by our abilities, by our development, and not by any less fundamental differences.

Here in our own country we have any number of attitudes which have become habits and which constitute our approach to the Jewish people, the Japanese and Chinese people, the German people, the Italian people, and above all, to the Negro people in our midst.

Perhaps because the Negroes are our largest minority, our attitude towards them will have to be faced first of all. I keep on repeating that the way to face this situation is by being completely realistic. We cannot force people to accept friends for whom they have no liking, but living in a democracy it is entirely reasonable to demand that every citizen of that democracy enjoy the fundamental rights of a citizen.

Over and over again, I have stressed the rights of every citizen:

Equality before the law.

Equality of education.

Equality to hold a job according to his ability.

Equality of participation through the ballot in the government.

These are inherent rights in a democracy, and I do not see how we can fight this war and deny these rights to any citizen in our own land.

The other relationships will gradually settle themselves once these major things are part of our accepted philosophy.

It seems trite to say to the Negro, you must have patience, when he has had patience so long; you must not expect miracles

Two champions of civil rights: ER with Mary McLeod Bethune

overnight, when he can look back to the years of slavery and say—how many nights! he has waited for justice. Nevertheless, that is what we must continue to say in the interests of our government as a whole and of the Negro people; but that does not mean that we must sit idle and do nothing. We must keep moving forward steadily, removing restrictions which have no sense, and fighting prejudice. If we are wise we shall do this where it is easiest to do at first, and watch it spread gradually to places where the old prejudices are slow to disappear.

There is now a great group of educated Negroes who can become leaders among their people, who can teach them the value of things of the mind and who qualify as the best in any field of endeavor. With these men and women it is impossible to think of any barriers of inferiority, but differences there are and always will be, and that is why on both sides there must be tact and patience and an effort at real understanding. Above everything else, no action must be taken which can cause so much bitterness that the whole liberalizing effort may be set back over a period of many years.

Public Questions and Her Answers

The following questions concerning public policy came to ER over the years, and these are the answers she gave. It is easy to see, in looking over them, the issues that troubled Americans during the Depression, World War II, and the Cold War. U.S. leadership in the world, organized labor, communism, education, medical plans, birth control, race relations, even the arts. It is also easy to see, in ER's answers, the way her mind worked and the public philosophy she followed.

* * *

There has been much talk about the United States taking the moral leadership in the building of the peace. What is your definition of moral leadership and how do you think we should go about assuming this responsibility? And if we fail in this leadership, what then?

Moral leadership is the quality in men and nations which makes other nations and leaders believe that they are not completely self-interested; that they have at heart the interests of other nations as well as of their own.

If confidence is once established in others and a belief in the honesty and general desire to bring about a peace which will wipe out economic as well as political rivalries of the kind which have plagued the world in the past, then I think that nation really will have established moral leadership.

If our nation fails, some other nation or group of nations may succeed. If no one succeeds, I think we are apt to have more wars and eventually wipe out our civilization.

Somebody has defined a liberal by calling him "a radical with a wife and two children." That definition doesn't satisfy me, and I can't think of any other which does—especially in these times. How would you state the liberal position?

It is very difficult to put into words the liberal position, but I would be inclined to say that a liberal tries to see a question from as many points of view as possible and then decide which is the point of view which will benefit the greatest number of people. He need not be either conservative or radical, but he must be able to be objective, to try to free himself from prejudice and to subordinate his own special interests to the interests of the people as a whole.

Why doesn't the government regulate labor unions as it does businesses and banks? Why shouldn't unions be compelled to publish audited financial statements and to hold annual open elections of officers? Labor would gain; only the dishonest labor leaders would lose.

To answer your question one has to consider, first of all, the collective bargaining power. This was not completely accepted even by our government until the passage of the National Labor Relations Act in 1936, and it has never been completely accepted by American industry.

Demands for complete regulation of labor unions probably arise out of the feeling that organized labor is irresponsible, but it has been proved over and over again that labor unions develop in direct proportion to employers' acceptance of unions and therefore of the principle of collective bargaining. Since business can choose for itself whether or not it shall incorporate, and it is never compelled to do so, to compel the incorporation of associations of workers who have banded together to protect their collective economy and welfare interests would be unfair, for they would be singled out for oppressive legislation when business was not.

This demand, I fear, often comes from the people who are really opposed to the workers' forming themselves into unions for protective purposes, and therefore would like to find a new and powerful weapon with which to destroy these organizations.

Individual unionists are liable for their acts, and the record of arrests made for even peaceful picketing proves beyond doubt that responsibility, while it may not be carried by the union as a whole, is certainly carried by each individual member of the union for whatever acts he may perform.

Most of the unions that I know publish a report of their financial status to their members, and do so in more accurate and simple form than do most business corporations. The reason that unions are not anxious to publish their financial statements for the benefit of the public is that when they are not well established, this information would inform employers immediately of certain of their weaknesses. All the well established unions within the CIO and in the AFL make public their financial statements.

I have found out that a man and woman who are my friends are active communists. They have a store. Knowing their sympathies, I have stopped patronizing them. However, the rest of the neighborhood continue to shop there, knowing they are communists. Am I doing wrong mixing business with politics?

Communists have a right to earn a living in the United States as long as we permit them to be here. We have an obligation to allow people to think and peacefully communicate their thoughts to others as long as they do not attempt to overthrow the Government by force. For that reason the fact that people who run stores and gain a livelihood believe in certain theories which we do not believe in is no reason, from my point of view, for not associating with them. It may, however, become disagreeable to have contacts with them because you feel you are helping them to promote something in which you do not believe. In that case, you will naturally not continue your contacts. That will be for personal reasons and not because of their political views only.

Would it not be possible to outlaw the Communist Party in the United States, although we are supposed to be a free country where everyone can express his convictions?

I think it would be highly unwise to outlaw the Communist Party in the United States. How would you feel if you were a citizen of the U.S.S.R. and decided that you preferred to have a more democratic form of government and you were outlawed because of it? That is practically what would happen to you in Russia today, but that has never happened to us in the United States. We are a free country, we can express our convictions with only the limitation of not advocating the overthrow of the Government by force. We can use all the persuasion that lies in our power. We trust, however, that democracy will so completely meet the needs of the people that there will always be among us people who believe strongly enough in it to fight for it with words and by deeds. We must prove that the people's well-being is satisfactory because of the way we use our democracy and that there is no value in making any change.

As mayor of our small city, my husband has been approached by the National Committee for American Education to head an investigation into the textbooks, teaching staff, and so on, of our local school system to discover, if any, and eradicate any subversive communist and socialist propaganda. What is your opinion of the National Committee for American Education?

'BUT IT WOULD MAKE SUCH A NICE SCOOP IF YOU'D ONLY
TELL ME, FRANKLIN.'

ER as a popular columnist with "inside information"

As I understand it, this committee was set up to screen textbooks
and to look into teaching staffs to prevent the teaching of subversive doctrines. My feeling about most of the screening processes
that are undertaken is that they are a type of censorship and should
be undertaken only when very essential and that the people charged
with such a duty should be carefully chosen. I have an instinctive

feeling that censorship is bad, particularly when it comes to censoring teachers. I think it may discourage any kind of liberal thought more often than it actually uncovers any communists. The communist is well enough trained to hide his opinions usually and to do his job in very indirect ways, but the liberal is apt to be forthright and inquiring and not always wary enough in biding his intellectual explorations from those who label all inquiry as subversive.

Why should we screen out of our schools knowledge of either socialism or communism? Socialism is increasingly accepted in a number of governments in Europe and Asia, and though we have accepted only some socialist ideas, it would be very unwise if we did not learn about them and weigh our own system and its results against these other systems. It is only by greater knowledge and conviction and enthusiasm that democracy can be made to meet the needs of the people. Our economic system has to be modified from time to time to meet new needs, and certainly our children should be trained to understand and to analyze and to compare all that we do with other systems and other results throughout the world. Academic freedom is something we cannot afford to endanger. There is a difference between studying something to know and understand and refute that which is false, and inculcating a particular line for the purpose of making a convert. That is really where the line should be drawn, and no one should be prevented from spreading knowledge among young or old on any legitimate subject. Calling anyone with a liberal or inquiring mind a communist or subversive person is a dangerous habit which has shown a tendency to increase in the United States of late.

Socialized medicine has been tried in England and France and in other countries under different systems of administration. What are your views on Government control in this field in the United States?

I believe the Government should improve its Public Health Service. I believe it could also aid in a better distribution of doctors in areas where at present there are none. I believe that the Government could aid in building hospitals and clinics where they are needed, by grants to communities. I do not know that we have found the best way of getting the best possible medical care for all our people. I think we should try whatever is suggested until we find that we have something which works well, because it is essential that medical care be accessible for all at a moderate cost where people can pay, and free where they cannot. A healthy nation is essential for future strength.

Considering the fact that millions of dollars are being spent, and thousands of individuals are devoting their energies and efforts to attempts to reduce the deaths of women and children in this country, do you think that any agency or group, religious or otherwise, has the right, in our democracy, to challenge these efforts by refusing to permit contraceptive advice to be given when medically indicated, thereby causing ill-health and even death among many of these mothers and their infants?

I do not think there is any agency or group, religious or otherwise, that would challenge any efforts to prevent ill-health among mothers and their infants. Contraceptive information should be available on a doctor's advice, but no one should be urged to use it. There seems to be a great deal of misunderstanding of what the whole planned parenthood program is.

It seems to me very foolish for anyone to stand against a thing which is so simple as the advisability of taking a doctor's advice and following out his directions. The Creator gave the power to human beings to continue their species on this earth, but he also gave them minds for use. Whatever is done by any human being should be done for the good of the human race, and certainly whatever will make babies healthier and mothers stronger in mind and in body, can do no harm to the future of the human race.

Do you believe in planned parenthood?

Yes, I do, if it is not used as an excuse to shirk having a family. I believe that every married couple should have children if they are able to do so, but I believe that they should use intelligence so that the children will be healthy and the mother not physically exhausted. Of course, if this is against your religious belief, that is a different matter, but outside of that it would seem sensible to plan intelligently for the family health and happiness.

My daughter is a student in one of the local high schools. Before the Junior Prom this year a Negro student asked if she expected to attend. When she said "No," he told her he would like to take her if she would go with him. She thanked him, but told him she had made other plans for the evening. What would be your reaction to such a situation? Would you permit your daughter to attend a Prom with a colored boy, or would you have felt, as I did, a little bit disconcerted at the idea of his even suggesting such a thing?

Your question is a difficult one to answer because there must be a background to it. If your daughter had known this young boy well, I do not think that it was in any way astonishing that he should ask her to go with him, because if they had been on a purely friendly acquaintanceship basis, there was no more reason why she should not go with him than with any one of the other boys whom she knew equally well.

What lies back of your feeling, of course, is the old fear of intermarriage between races. That is something I feel we have to deal with on an entirely different basis from mere friendly association. There may come a time when it will seem as natural to marry a man from any race, or any part of the world, as it will to marry your next-door neighbor. We haven't reached that time as yet, and there is still considerable feeling when people marry who have different religious backgrounds, and there is, of course, more feeling still about intermarriage between different races. So it seems to me that that question has to be dealt with individually, by families, by individuals and by society. At present intermarriage between races, and even between people of different religions, often brings reprisals from society and from families, which make for great unhappiness. Anyone undertaking such a marriage must have a full realization of what she is actually facing.

However, going to a prom is like any other casual thing which you do; and if we are not going to be able to have ordinary contacts with people who are citizens of our own country, how on earth can we expect that we will be able to have the same kind of contact with people who live in different parts of the world? I think we can have peace in our hearts and real friendship for people even though there may still be some fundamental reason why we would not marry. Therefore, if I were you I would not worry too much about the people with whom your daughter dances. I should hope that she could be unconsciously friendly with all her associates in school, and I would be rather proud that a boy of another race felt that he could ask your daughter to go to a prom—which shows, I think, that her attitude has been kind and mature.

Americans have often been accused of an attitude of apathy toward the arts. In view of this fact, would you be in favor of our government subsidizing young artists so that a greater amount of art would be available to a larger number of American people?

All young civilizations are slow to recognize the value of their artists. I think we are beginning to grow up in the United States of

America, however and some of our cities and states are accepting a certain amount of responsibility for the development of different art expressions.

I hope that nationally we will accept this responsibility before long and perhaps make available through our public school system, or in some other way, the development of young artists in a variety of the arts.

HER OPINIONS ON PERSONAL MATTERS

Readers and friends also asked ER many questions of a personal nature—that is, questions about how to solve the problems in their personal lives. The essays she wrote and the answers she gave reflect not only her intense interest and concern for the problems of others but how often they paralleled her own personal problems and difficulties.

An Essay on How to Deal with Criticism

ER was the most criticized—as well as the most admired—First Lady in American history. Her detractors found fault with her liberal philosophy, with her willingness to speak out on issues that concerned her, her unwillingness to act the part of a "lady" as some of them understood the term, even her appearance, her voice, and the behavior of her children. The criticism, particularly its often virulent language and tone, must have hurt her. In an article for *Ladies Home Journal* for November 1944, she addressed the issue of criticism and how to deal with it.

"HOW TO TAKE CRITICISM"

One of the things which my critics most frequently stress is the fact that I am not elected to any office; therefore, I can have no sense of responsibility, they say, since no one elected or appointed me to any office, so it is clear that I must be seeking publicity.

Let me disabuse them of that idea. People who live in a goldfish bowl cannot escape publicity. It is obvious that the President's wife is not an elected official, but she has certain obligations. First, there is the obligation to run the President's house, his official house, the White House, paying due attention to all the rules and regulations which custom and the law lay down for the running of that house, which belongs to the people of the United States.

This is an obligation on which there is little difference of opinion; and if I confined myself to giving parties, even in wartime, my critics would be few, I imagine—though one cannot be sure!

The differences arise in regard to other activities. As the President's wife, a great many people throughout the United States think that you can get information for them, which they cannot get themselves, or help them to accomplish certain things which they cannot accomplish themselves. In both of these situations they are quite correct, sometimes, in appealing to you, and you are able without any impropriety to get them information, and sometimes to impart the information they give you to the proper people.

There is one area, however, where criticism of any individual would be entirely valid. A good many people think that because of your husband's position you can exert influence to obtain favors which they could not obtain on their own merits. If you did this, you would quite rightly be criticized. All you can do with propriety is to give the facts as you know them to the proper officials and leave them free to investigate and proceed as they see fit.

In the natural course of events, however, you get to know a good deal about the country and its people, and conditions and situations as they exist. This gives you an opportunity, perhaps, to be of service, and here is where criticism centers.

Should the President's wife, who is not elected to office, be interested in working conditions, for instance? She has rare opportunities for knowing about them if she has eyes, ears, and understanding. Should she be blind, deaf, and dumb?

There is no question about it—all criticism is entirely permissible. There are no laws as to your conduct; you are a citizen, free like any other, so you live by your own judgments, tastes and conscience. Hence the question is:

"How much attention should the individual criticized pay to criticism?"

No human being enjoys being disliked, so it would be normal to try to avoid actions which bring criticism. When it comes to deciding whether you will be a Dresden-china figure, daintily placed on the mantelpiece, and thus avoid any criticism; or lead a strictly personal life when the world is rocking as an independent citizen of the United States, considering it your duty to use such opportunities as come your way for service as you see it, then the decision, for certain people, will be easy. They will do and be damned; but the others, who won't do, what of them? You might expect them to be praised, but that is not the way it works in many cases. In these situations you're damned if you do and damned if you don't!

In the last analysis, you have to be friends with yourself twenty-four hours of the day. If you run counter to others now and then, you have enemies; but life would become unbearable if you thought about it all the time, so you have to ignore the critics. You know quite well, when you face audiences and are among crowds of people, that perhaps everybody present dislikes you cordially. Then you do your best to make others see your point of view; but if you cannot win them over, you still must go on your way, because each human being has an obligation to do what seems right according to his own conscience. If you are honest, you will always be your own most severe critic.

There are two kinds of criticism which come to us all in this world. One is constructive criticism.

To be really constructive, criticism must come to us from people whom we know and whose judgment we trust and who we feel really care, not only for us as individuals but for the things which may be affected by the actions or attitudes which we take.

Destructive criticism is always valueless, and anyone with common sense soon becomes completely indifferent to it. It may, of course, be cruel at times. Sometimes it may be unjust and bring the individual a certain amount of bitterness, but I think any sensible person soon learns to recover from the bitterness and to ignore the cruelty.

To do anything constructive or creative in this world, people must have some self-confidence. Therefore, other people who love them must always be careful, even in giving their honest criticism and opinions, not to destroy completely an individuals faith in his own judgment.

* * *

The people who love you may help you greatly, however, with some types of criticism. People whom you have never met, but whom you admire, can through their example give you inspiration, and frequently what they are and what they do and say will form the basis on which you criticize your own actions.

To spend your life, however, thinking about "what will be said" would result in a completely unprofitable and embittering existence. Since one of the chief things that human beings can do to be helpful in life is to be cheerful, it would indeed be foolish to dwell upon the criticism of those who can know little about you, who do not take the trouble to verify their facts, and who frequently have ulterior motives for the things which they say or write.

I think it is salutary to read criticisms, even unkind and untrue ones. I do when they happen to come my way in the natural course of events. I do not seek them out, but they certainly tend to keep one from being overconfident or getting what is commonly known as the "swelled head"; but all of us must be wary not to have our confidence in ourselves completely destroyed, or we will be unable to do anything. Some criticisms I read and forget. Some remain with me and have been very valuable because I know they were kindly meant and honest and I admired and believed in the integrity of the people who expressed their convictions, which were opposed to mine.

I would not want the people I love and who are most often with me to withhold criticism; but since those are the people you must count on for giving you the courage to live with a purpose, they are the ones who have the greatest responsibility to make their criticism constructive, since they know you will pay attention to them.

Sometimes criticisms I have read have seemed unjustified and unkind, and sometimes they have annoyed or hurt me, but I learned long ago that the world is not based on universal justice! One should expect it, so I think that I have developed a great indifference, except where people in whom I believe are involved.

I can honestly say that I hate no one; and perhaps the best advice I can give to anyone who suffers from criticism, and yet must in the public eye, would be contained in the words of my aunt, Mrs. William Cowles. She was President Theodore Roosevelt's sister, and the aunt to whom many of the young people in the family went for advice. I had asked her whether I should do something which at the time caused a great deal of criticism, and her answer was:

"Do not be bothered by what people say as long as you are sure that you are doing what seems right to you, but be sure that you face yourself honestly."

Friendship with oneself is all-important because without it one cannot be in the world.

So be your own critic!

Personal Questions and Her Answers

Most of the people who wrote asking ER personal questions were women; and their primary concern seemed to be relations with the men in their lives, their husbands, their sons, their husbands' mothers, their sons' wives. Without referring to her own experience, ER advised women about unfaithful husbands and obtrusive mothers-in-law.

* * *

What do you consider the three most important qualifications of a good husband?

That he shall be honest, not only in material things, but in intellectual things; that he shall be capable of real love; and that he shall find the world an increasingly interesting place in which to live every day of his life.

My husband says he has a right to have an affair with another woman when he's overseas. When I ask him if I have the same kind of rights he says no, I'm the mother of children and have to be respectable. It's not that I want an affair with another man, but I don't think his attitude is right. Do you?

Of course what your husband is trying to guard against is the feeling of guilt which comes to any man who has been physically unfaithful to the woman whom he really loves and does not want to lose. The act of being physically unfaithful seems much less important to the average man, and he finds it hard to understand why the woman he loves looks upon it as all-important. Yet, as you prove by your question to him, if a woman tries to take the same point of view a husband is quite horrified and turns to the old code of respectability on the woman's part for the sake of the children. How about respectability on the man's part being of value to the children?

There is something more, however, that should be said on this whole question, since physical faithfulness is perhaps more difficult for men than for women. I imagine your husband, who apparently does love you, is trying to make sure that you will not turn away from him if anything of the kind should happen while he is overseas. You and he will have to decide what is the right attitude to take. Nobody else can decide it for you.

I married a widower. The first thing I saw when I entered my new home was the picture of his first wife prominently displayed on the mantelpiece. He still goes to the cemetery to mourn her, carrying flowers, especially on days meaningful to his first marriage. What is the sensible attitude for each of us to display?

When you married a widower you knew he had had a first wife. In all probability you hoped that he had loved his first wife, because the fact that he had been able to love her would make it probable that he would love you.

The fact that he is still loyal to her memory and still mourns her is something you should be happy about. If you had known her you probably would join with him in thinking of her. As long as you had not known her you cannot do that, but you can at least respect and admire him for his loyalty and realize that in a different way he will give you more just because of this loyalty.

No one loves two people in exactly the same way, but one may love two people equally and yet differently. And if you love one person very much you will love another person perhaps even more because you have learned how to love and what love can mean.

Be happy with your husband in the kind of love he gives you and be grateful for his loyalty to the past, because it augurs well for his loyalty to the present.

My husband's mother is coming to live with us. She has lived by herself far away for a long time and has been extremely unhappy and lonely. We have had an unusually happy marriage and I have a happy disposition, but when she's here I find it is all I can do to keep from displaying ill temper and being depressed. She and my husband seem so happy together and I feel like a wet blanket and finally lose confidence in myself. My husband is a fine man with a strong character. I have three lovely sons—one a small baby. I want to do a good job in bringing up our children. How can I learn to relax and to have positive thinking about this? Is there anything I can read that will help?

If I were you, I would have a talk with your mother-in-law and with your husband, together or separately, as you find easier, but I would tell them both the same things: namely, that somehow a way must be found in which you can be included in the pleasures they find in their mutual companionship. You must, of course, make an effort to be companionable. If your mother-in-law is going to live with you, definite rules as regards the children should be decided on. You must have the final say-so, and there must be no effort to sabotage your discipline or your position with the children. Grandmothers can be a great help, but they can also be a heartrending burden to their daughters-in-law, and only honesty between all concerned can save that situation. Honestly talking over things and not repressing your feelings, but making an effort to be kind and spontaneous in your contacts, will, I hope, bring you success.

My boys are married and live not far from us in the same city, yet there are weeks at a time when I do not see them or talk to them unless I call them up. I'm certain they love me and yet they are unconsciously negligent. I don't want to put it on a "duty" basis and I try every way to be the kind of mother a married man wants. What do you advise?

If I were you, when I wanted to talk to my boys or their wives, I would call them on the telephone and I would try to make some kind of regular weekly arrangement with them. Perhaps you could have lunch or supper together on Sundays, but do not make them feel that they can never break the engagement. Sometimes it is easier to do something that you can count on and know is going to happen, which will bring you together and keep the family spirit alive.

The young people are busy and have many interests of their own and it is harder for them to find the time to call you than it is for you to call them. I would not do it too often, but once or twice a week would show you are interested and want to keep in touch.

Do you agree that a girl should hide her intellectual side if she's going to be popular with boys?

No. What is the use of being liked by people whom you do not like? If you hide the things in which you are really interested in order to please people of different interests, you are not going to have friends with whom you can be natural, and that seems to me a very foolish way to live. I think, however, that if a girl boasts of her knowledge everyone will laugh at her. Just be perfectly natural and talk about the things that interest you with people who have similar interests. Then you will have friends that you will enjoy and who will enjoy you.

Do you think it is true, "A son is a son until he gets a wife, but a daughter is a daughter all her life"? Most people, I find, do; but I think a son can never be as close to a mother as a daughter. I don't feel his marriage has anything to do with it.

I think this is a question of individuals entirely. I have known many sons who were devoted to their parents and who remained close and as devoted after they were married as they had been before. Naturally a man has to give more time to supporting and living with his family when he has one, and he will not be quite as free, perhaps, to be with his parents, but closeness does not imply constant association. A daughter when she is married is in exactly the same position as a son: she has a family of her own which she has to look after; but again I have known many daughters to stay close to their parents.

The real answer, of course, is the quality of the relationship that exists between parents and children, and it may exist with either a son or a daughter, or it may exist with both sons and daughters in a family, and marriage does not have to change it.

HER OPINIONS ON PRIVATE MATTERS

People also asked ER about her own life, and the questions were often both intimate and intrusive. Doubtless she avoided answering those questions that threatened to cause her pain or that she felt the public did not need to know; but it is amazing how many such private questions she did publicly address. In many cases, if with our present knowledge of her life we read between the lines, we find her answering much more candidly that we might expect.

An Essay on Why She Did Not Run for Office

Soon after FDR died, many of her admirers encouraged her to run for public office, some said for the United States Senate, some said for Vice-President, some even said for President, in 1948. In the following article published in *Look* on July 9, 1946, she may not have revealed all of her thoughts on the subject, but she gave the public a frank and open answer to the questions.

"WHY I DO NOT CHOOSE TO RUN"

There has been some curiosity as to why I am not knocking at the door of the members of my political party, who make up the slates for candidates for office, in order to obtain a nomination for some elective office.

At first I was surprised that anyone should think that I would want to run for office, or that I was fitted to hold office. Then I realized that some people felt that I must have learned something from my husband in all the years that he was in public life! They also knew that I had stressed the fact that women should accept responsibility as citizens.

I heard that I was being offered the nomination for governor or for the United States Senate in my own state, and even for Vice President. And some particularly humorous souls wrote in and suggested that I run as the first woman President of the United States!

The simple truth is that I have had my fill of public life of the more or less stereotyped kind. I do believe that every citizen, as long as he is alive and able to work, has an obligation to work on public questions and that he should choose the kind of work he is best fitted to do.

Therefore, when I was offered an opportunity to serve on the United Nations organization, I accepted it. I did this, not because I really wanted to go to London last January, but because it seemed as though I might be able to use the experiences of a lifetime and make them valuable to my nation and to the people of the world at this particular time. I knew, of course, how much my husband hoped that, out of the war, an organization for peace would really develop.

It was not just to further my husband's hopes, however, that I agreed to serve in this particular way. It was rather that I myself had always believed that women might have a better chance to bring about the understanding necessary to prevent future wars if they could serve in sufficient number in these international bodies.

The plain truth, I am afraid, is that in declining to consider running for the various public offices which have been suggested to me, I am influenced by the thought that no woman has, as yet, been able to build up and hold sufficient backing to carry through a program. Men and women both are not yet enough accustomed to following a woman and looking to her for leadership. If I were young enough it might be an interesting challenge, and we have some women in Congress who may carry on this fight.

However, I am already an elderly woman, and I would have to start in whatever office I might run for as a junior with no weight of experience in holding office behind me. It seems to me that fairly young men and women should start holding minor offices and work up to other important ones, developing qualifications for holding these offices as they work.

I have been an onlooker in the field of politics. In some ways I hope I have occasionally been a help, but always by doing things which I was particularly fitted by my own background and experience to do. My husband was skilled in using people and, even though I was his wife, I think he used me in his career as he used other people. I am quite sure that Louis Howe, who was one of the most astute politicians as well as one of the most devoted of friends, trained me and used me for the things which he thought I could do well, but always in connection with my husband's career.

In the last years of his life Louis Howe used to ask me if I had any ambitions to hold political office myself. I think he finally became convinced that though I understood the worst and the best of politics and statesmanship, I had absolutely no desire to participate in it.

For many years of my life I realized that what my husband was attempting to do was far more important than anything which I could possibly accomplish; and therefore I never said anything, or wrote anything, without first balancing it against the objectives which I thought he was working for at the time. We did not always agree as to methods, but our ultimate objectives were fortunately very much the same.

Never in all the years can I remember his asking me not to say or to write anything, even though we occasionally argued very vehemently and sometimes held diametrically opposite points of view on things of the moment.

I think my husband probably often used me as a sounding board, knowing that my reactions would be the reactions of the average man and woman in the street.

My husband taught me that one cannot follow blindly any line which one lays down in advance, because circumstances will mod-ify one's thinking and one's action. And in the last year since his death I have felt sure that our objectives would remain very much the same. But I have known that I was free and under compulsion to say and to do the things which I, as an individual, believed on the questions of the day. In a way it has lifted a considerable weight from my shoulders, feeling that now, when I speak, no one will attribute my thoughts to someone holding an important office and whose work may be hurt and helped thereby. If people do not like what I say nowadays, they can blame me, but it will hurt no one else's plans or policies.

There is freedom in being responsible only to yourself which I would now find it hard to surrender in taking a party office. I believe that the Democratic Party, at least the progressive part of the Democratic Party, represents the only safe way we have of moving forward in this country. I believe that the liberal-minded Democrats hold to the only international policy which can bring us a peaceful world. I will work for the candidates of my party when I think they offer the best there is in the field of public ser-vice, and I will even accept mediocre men now and then if I feel that the rank and file of the Party is strong enough in its beliefs to make those inadequate leaders do better than their own ability gives promise of in the way of achievement.

However, if I do not run for office, I am not beholden to my Party. What I give, I give freely and I am too old to want to be curtailed in any way in the expression of my own thinking.

To be entirely honest I will have to confess that I thought at first one of my reasons might be that I did not want to engage in the rough and tumble of a political campaign. This, of course, would be rank self-indulgence and I should be the last one to allow myself to decline to run for public office because of any such reason, since I have urged on other women the need for developing a less sensitive spirit and for learning to give and take as men do.

I do not think that this consideration really enters into my decision. I have lived long in a goldfish bowl, and my husband's death does not seem in any way to have altered the attacks which come upon one from certain quarters. So I do not think that running for office would have brought me any more of the disagreeable things which we must learn to endure. In the long run, the mass of the people are likely to form a fairly truthful estimate of people who are before them in public life.

Had I wanted to run for office, therefore, I imagine in many ways I could have stood up under all types of attack and suffered less than most people. But I could rather help others, younger people, whose careers lie ahead of them and who have years in which to achieve their objectives. What I do may still be important, but it won't last long enough.

In the meantime, I shall be glad to serve wherever my past experiences seem to fit me to do a specific job.

Many people will think that these are all very inadequate answers and that when you are told that you might be useful, you should accept the judgment of others and go to work. All I can say in reply is that during a long life I have always done what, for one reason or another, was the thing which was incumbent upon me to do without any consideration as to whether I wished to do it or not. That no longer seems to be a necessity, and for my few remaining years I hope to be free!

Private Questions and Her Answers

People asked ER all kinds of questions about her private life, about her sons' education, whether she had black ancestors, why she did not run for President; and she seemed not to ignore even the most intimate.

* * *

If you and your husband believed in democracy so sincerely, why did you send your children to private schools?

Because in both my husband's family and in my family there was a tradition which made it seem natural to send the boys to Groton. Their father had gone there, their grandfathers had held the belief that if you could afford it, you should pay for your children's education as well as paying in taxes for the education of other children whose parents were not so well off.

I have thought for many years that that theory is one of doubtful validity. I believe our public schools would be better if people who really wished to see their children obtain the best possible education were personally and vitally concerned in public schools.

There is value in private schools when they develop new techniques of teaching and make educational experiments. In addition, of course, it is possible to give very much more individual attention to children and to limit the size of classes and occasionally to develop individual abilities as they are discovered. I think this could be done, however, if the need were recognized, in public schools; and though it is still a debatable question, I think it is one which should be carefully considered and debated even more than it is at present.

Very careful decisions should be made as to why we send children to private schools. Some children, without question, should go to public schools and will do better there. Others might need what private schools have to offer; but that this decision should be made purely on whether a family is able to pay for it or not seems to me very questionable, and this is recognized by the private schools, for they are giving more and more scholarships.

In the postwar world I hope we can make our public schools better than they have been in the past; and if private schools continue to function, they should have clearly defined objectives.

I don't mean to be rude, but do you have colored blood in your family, as you seem to derive so much pleasure from associating with colored folks? Would you approve of one of your children having as a most intimate friend a colored person?

I only know about all my ancestors as far back as their arrival in this country, but I do know in certain cases where they came from and where they lived before coming here.

I haven't as yet discovered during that period any colored blood, but, of course, if any of us go back far enough, I suppose we can find that we all stem from the same beginnings. I have no feeling that the colored race is inferior to the white race. Given the same opportunities over several generations, they have produced artists, scientists, educators, and many valuable citizens. I would certainly have no objection if a child of mine chose a friend among the peoples of any race, regardless of color or creed.

Did your husband notice a new dress or hat when you wore one, or was he like so many other men who never even see a wife's new clothes?

I think my husband was too preoccupied, usually, to notice my clothes, but sometimes he would suddenly look up and say he liked something I had been wearing for two or three years!

How do you keep from worrying?

By trust in God and self-discipline which has been forced on me over a long period of years. Even at that I do not always succeed in not worrying, but I manage to hide my worries as a rule.

You—having had an excellent background, a wonderful education, an unlimited amount of parliamentary experience, so many years in the White House, so many positions of note, and having had an honest political career all your life, with a real human heart—why then do you not do the world a favor by running for the office of President of the United States, thereby becoming the first female President and demonstrating what a Roosevelt can do?

You credit me, my dear lady, with more qualifications than I believe I have. You also forget that I am 68 years of age and that I have no desire to be President of the United States.

I do not think the time has come for a woman to be President of the United States. It seems to me that before a woman can successfully be President many more public offices must be filled by women and we in this country must have ceased to think of our candidates as men or women but only as people who have the proper qualifications for the job to which we are considering electing them.

On the whole I think the Roosevelts have already demonstrated what they can do, and probably will do so many times again, but I do not think it is up to me to demonstrate either the capacities of Roosevelts or women in general. I feel at the present time that a woman could not fill the Presidency successfully because she might not be able to hold a following long enough, and without a loyal following she could accomplish little.

This last question and its answer may at first seem more public than private. But knowing what we now do about the relationship of Eleanor and Franklin Roosevelt, it takes on great private significance as well.

What do you think of the present divorce laws in the U.S.A.?
Do you not think it would make for a better social order if there was one uniform divorce law for the whole country?
While most people seem to agree on these questions, nothing seems to be done about them and they are certainly pointed up by the recent Supreme Court decision.

I think they could be improved.

I think one uniform divorce law would be better but only if we recognize that there are a number of reasons for which divorce should be granted. For instance, incompatibility may be just as devastating to a happy marriage in some cases as infidelity. I imagine the reason that nothing is actually done when so many people talk about these questions, is that they are very difficult questions to decide.

It is perfectly evident that every effort should be made, once a marriage is consummated and children are born, to make that marriage a success, but it is also evident that sometimes, even with very great effort, a marriage fails and children brought up in homes where there is no real marriage sometimes have a more unhappy time than if their parents had separated.

QUESTIONS FOR RESPONSIVE ESSAYS

1. What assumptions does Eleanor Roosevelt make in writing her *Moral Basis for Democracy*? In what ways are her ideas traditional and in what ways are they new? What changes in American society did she advocate, and what groups did she believe needed special attention? Why?

2. What problems of democracy does she ignore? What problems of morality does she ignore? Is she idealistic or realistic? Is she naive? How much does her philosophy of government offer us today?

3. What do the articles she wrote and the answers she gave to people's questions tell you about ER's public philosophy? What were her interests, and how deeply does she appear to have thoughts about them? What did she contribute to the national debate in her day? What might her opinions offer national debate in our day?

4. What do her articles and answers tell you about how she approached her own personal problems and those of others? What did she tell the American people about how to survive a depression, a world war, and the tensions of a cold war? Which of her opinions are valuable to people today?

5. What does she reveal about her private life in articles and answers addressed to questions asked about herself? What does she tell and what does she hide? How would a First Lady today answer such questions differently? Would any other approach be as effective as ER's approach?

6. How was ER viewed by the Americans who wrote to her with their questions? How was she to them a traditional First Lady, and how had she made the position new?

PART V

A Woman First

The stories of Elizabeth Cady Stanton, Dr. Anna Shaw, Susan B. Anthony and Carrie Chapman Catt are inspiring reading. They felt this power given to women would herald great changes for the good of mankind.

—ELEANOR ROOSEVELT
Autobiography, 1961

She talks like a social worker and acts like a feminist.

—RUBY BLACK
Associated Press article, 1933

High on the list of causes that ER espoused and championed during the New Deal, World War II, her years at the United Nations, and until her death in 1962 was the advancement of women. As the best known and most influential woman in America and then in the world, she used her prestige and prominence to encourage women to achieve their full potential, to show them by example how they might more effectively exercise their legal rights, and to help them gain positions of leadership and responsibility where they could refine and demonstrate their skills.

Historians argue over whether ER should be called a feminist. She did not exhibit all the characteristics of the feminists who came after her death. Although she permitted herself to rise in political influence as far as her times would allow and accept, although she saw to it that more women were placed in governmental authority than ever before, she seemed not to resent continuing male leadership, so long as it was reasoned and considerate. Although she believed that women should' take places of leadership as soon as they were individually ready to do so, although she held news conferences "for women only" so that agencies had to hire more women reporters, she seemed in no great hurry for a woman to be President, and she quickly discouraged efforts to push her toward that goal. Although she chose to have a public career alongside her marriage, she seemed not to doubt that for most women marriage and children is the most natural state.

While she may or may not be called a feminist, she was by the standards of her day a forward-looking woman. She enjoyed the very public life she lived; she relished exercising political power and influence, and she encouraged women to follow her example and to think and act for themselves. She was in every sense of the word an advocate for women's rights. In fact, the last public assignment she accepted, the year she died, was to head President John Kennedy's Commission on the Status of Women. She was many things, but she was a woman first.

When ER reached the age of 21 in 1905, women in America did not even have the right to vote. As wife of the Assistant Secretary of the Navy during World War I, she still could not vote; and no woman held any important office in the U.S. government. She was 36 when she was first permitted to vote, along with other women, following the adoption of the Nineteenth Amendment to the Constitution. Yet by the time of her death women had served in the President's Cabinet, on federal commissions, as ambassadors, and at the United Nations. They could realistically dream of being President. Much of this progress for women was due to her own example and efforts.

At the age of 75, as she went painstakingly back over her life in order to write her autobiography, she remembered all the steps of her climb from the sheltered, naive, rather oppressed early role of wife and mother to ever higher levels of personal, social, and professional fulfillment:

> My chief objective, as a girl, was to do my duty. This had been drilled into me as far back as I could remember. Not my duty as I saw it, but my duty as laid down for me by other people. It never occurred to me to revolt. Anyhow, my one overwhelming need in those days was to be approved, to be loved, and I did whatever was required of me, hoping it would bring me nearer to the approval and love I so much wanted.

As a young woman, my sense of duty remained as strict and rigid as it had been when I was a girl, but it had changed its focus. My husband and my children became the center of my life and their needs were my new duty. I am afraid now that I approached this new obligation much as I had my childhood duties. I was still timid, still afraid of doing something wrong, of making mistakes, of not living up to the standards required by my mother-in-law, of failing to do what was expected of me.

As a result, I was so hidebound by duty that I became too critical, too much of a disciplinarian. I was so concerned with bringing up my children properly that I was not wise enough just to love them. Now, looking back, I think I would rather spoil a child a little and have more fun out of it.

It was not until I reached middle age that I had the courage to develop interests of my own, outside of my duties to my family. In the beginning, it seems to me now, I had no goal beyond the interests themselves, in learning about people and conditions and the world outside our own United States. Almost at once I began to discover that interests leads to interest, knowledge leads to more knowledge, the capacity for understanding grows with the effort to understand.

From that time on, though I have had many problems, though I have known the grief and the loneliness that are the lot of most human beings, though I have had to make and still have to make endless adjustments, I have never been bored, never found the days long enough for the range of activities with which I wanted to fill them. And, having learned to stare down fear, I long ago reached the point where there is no living person whom I fear, and few challenges that I am not willing to face.

SELECTIONS FROM
IT'S UP TO THE WOMEN,
WRITTEN IN 1933, DURING HER
FIRST YEAR AS FIRST LADY

By the time FDR was elected President in 1932, after a decade of training herself for public life, ER was aware of her worth as a woman and now of her power as First Lady. She began teaching herself to write, as she had taught herself to make speeches, in order to reach as wide an audience as possible. It was not an easy task for a busy woman of forty-eight, but she kept at it. It is significant that her first book, published in 1933, addressed "our obligations as women to the new social order that is growing up around us."

It's up to the Women, which launched her career as a writer of books, articles, essays, and columns, discussed the role she hoped women would play in every part of American life. The selections that follow analyze (1) the choices women have regarding family and careers, and (2) the opportunities and responsibilities women have in public affairs. It is significant that she wrote more fervently on these topics than when she recounted the impressive accomplishments of her own life.

Nowadays there is a great deal of agitation as to whether married women should work or not and in order to consider the question, I think we should go back a little bit further and consider whether women should work at all.

There was a time when very few women worked outside of their homes. All women were brought up with the feeling that a woman's place was in the home. She must marry, and if she did not marry, she had no work in the world, and we have in many old novels a picture of the maiden lady left to live at home, being more or less of a drudge, whiling away her time looking after the younger members of the family with very little attention from anybody, and having all her work accepted as a matter of course in return for the kindness of the man of the family who provided her with food and lodging.

This is not a pretty picture nor one that we like to contemplate but we must have it in our minds when we discuss the modern status of women, even though there were many instances of happy maiden aunts and cousins who were happy and beloved. From this condition the women have gradually risen in consideration largely as they gained economic independence for themselves and could provide financial help in the homes. For some time, of course, it has been necessary for the girl in many families to go to work at a fairly early age. Nowadays an effort is being made to keep young people a little longer out of the working field. This affects women as it does men, but more and more women are going to work every year and because of that we must look upon it not as an academic question, but as an actual situation which is with us to stay in the industrial world and in the average family.

Even where the young girl could be supported at home, she wants to register her own personality and to develop her own interests, and she spends for her clothes or for some interest of her own a part of the money which she is able to earn. Usually every girl pays part of her earnings for food and lodging even when she lives at home, and many a girl puts in all that she earns to support not only herself but some other members of her family. If it is not a father or a mother, it may be the education of some younger brother or sister that she is carrying.

I never like to think of this subject of a woman's career and a woman's home as being a controversy. It seems to me perfectly obvious that if a woman falls in love and marries, of course her first interest and her first duty is to her home, but her duty to her home does not of necessity preclude her having another occupation. A woman, just like a man, may have a great gift for some particular thing. That does not mean that she must give up the joy of marrying and having a home and children. It simply means, when we set them in opposition to each other, that we haven't as yet grown accustomed to the fact that women's lives must be adjusted and arranged for in just the same way that men's lives are. Women may have to sacrifice certain things at times—so do men.

When the keeping of a home took all the strength and time that a woman had, the home was the factory where much that we now buy ready-made had to be manufactured. Few of us realize that only a little over a hundred years ago all the candles and soap and food used by the household in winter as well as in summer were prepared by the women of the house; all the linen and all the wool were made in the home; practically all the clothes both for men and women were made at home; all the washing was done at home.

I have a piece of linen made in Duchess County from flax that was grown in the county and nowadays the art is completely lost. The necessity has gone to-day and therefore there are few women who have been in this country more than a short time and whose husbands earn more than the bare necessities of life, who are not able to do something beside keeping their home. They may choose to play bridge, or golf, or they may choose to do some part-time work or even full-time work in some job that interests them. If so—the only people to be concerned about it are the members of the family. To be sure, sometimes children resent the fact that their mother has a job and is not at their beck and call at any hour of the day or night. This is only so, of course, when her work is not needed for the necessities of life. But granted that the father provides the necessities, sometimes the children are jealous of the fact that a mother should want any interests outside of theirs. They are justified if something really vital goes out of their lives, but if their physical needs are cared for and if their mother, on her return, has enough vitality to keep in touch with their daily lives and know what has happened to them and to give them her sympathetic interest and advice, then it is probably better for the future lives of these children that they should have to exercise a little unselfishness, a little thought for themselves and for others because their mother is not always on hand. They have a right to expect that if they have a problem she will listen to it, but they have no right to expect that she will give up that which she loves and which is constructive and creative work, because they would like to have her home at five o'clock instead of at six o'clock. It might be fair to ask her to give up pure recreation but not a thing which really makes her an individual.

Do not make the mistake of thinking when you are married you need make no further effort about your family relations. The very best thing that comes to a woman with a job is the fact that she has to use her brains in order to find time for both her job and her home duties. This keeps her brain from stagnating. She has something new to talk to her husband about and he never will get the feeling that she is just like the old chair which he has always sat in—comfortable, but thoroughly familiar and never very interesting in consequence. The job of being a home-keeper, a wife and a mother plus some other job or some other work is quite a job. If any woman has the health and vitality and the desire to do both, it seems to me that it ought to make for a happier relationship at home instead of a discontented one.

In the emergency we are passing through, however, I am getting enumerable appeals asking that married women be not allowed to hold jobs which might be filled by married men or single men and women. That point of view is perhaps necessary during an emergency and it may be necessary for a woman to relinquish voluntarily her work if the man is earning enough for the family to love on, but as a permanent concession to the needs of society I rebel, for it seems to me that we have built up our nation on the theory that work is honorable; that those who can do something creative and productive may be doing some intangible good to their own souls, which, if they were not allowed to express themselves in work, might mean a loss to themselves in enrichment of personality, and in their happiness, and therefore, in the end, a loss to the community at large.

The problem is always an individual one which every woman must decide for herself, but if a woman wants to work and keep her home, let me beg you, Mr. Man, to help her and not hold her back. If you are sympathetic and understanding, you will find her in the end a better helpmate and your cooperation will mean a better and happier understanding between you. If you fight her she may be resentful, though she may give in to you, and you may wake up some day to find that you have a wife in your home who is an automaton—no longer a fulfilled and happy personality.

* * *

Of course, the mother who takes entire charge of her own children will not be able to work at a steady job which takes her outside of her home. If, however she is able to bring up her children and care for them herself, I can think of nothing which will probably bring her greater happiness and be more valuable to them, but there are many, many women who do not naturally and happily spend day after day with little children. There is no use in closing your eyes to the fact that women do not become satisfactory nurses and governesses simply because they have brought children into the world.

It may be far better for the children to have a woman actually taking care of them who may never have had a child. There should be between a mother and a child a bond deeper and greater than that which comes in any other relationship and I think that most mothers have a kind of unselfish love which makes them willing to try to understand and help their children, but this doesn't mean that they are wise disciplinarians or can carry out the proper daily routine to give a child a healthy body and a disciplined character.

In the next passage she took up the subject of women's right to vote and participate in the political system:

There is one new activity which entered the life of women with the passage of the Nineteenth Amendment in 1918. With the right to vote, a whole new field of responsibility and direct power came into the hands of the women of the country. A few of our states had already given women the right to vote and in some communities they were allowed to vote in school elections, but they did not enjoy the full privileges of citizenship as the equals of men throughout the whole country until 1918.

* * *

Fourteen years have now gone by and everywhere people are asking, "What have the women done with the vote?" I often wonder why they don't ask the men the same question, but I realize that it is a high compliment to women that evidently they were expected to bring about some marked change in political conditions, and so I would like to look into the question of women as citizens and see just what we have done and are doing and then perhaps dream a little about what we may do in the future.

The vast majority of women, like the vast majority of men, have little time to give to anything but the earning of their daily bread either by actually working themselves or by caring for home and children and making other people's earnings go as far as possible. Their good citizenship consists in leading their lives so as to make them as productive of good for all around them as they can be, and their public duty is expressed by using their vote as intelligently as possible.

A vote is never an intelligent vote when it is cast without knowledge. Just doing what some one else tells you do to without any effort to find out what the facts are for yourself is being a poor citizen. When women first had the vote, many of them did not know how to get information on questions of government. Others had seen the men of years go and vote, had heard them talk a little during the weeks just before election about this or that candidate or this or that party, but had never gathered that there was much concern for the things the parties stood for. You were a Democrat or a Republican because your family belonged to one or to the other party, because you people had been in the north or in the south at the time of the War Between the States, or because it was easier to get advancement in business in your locality if you belonged to one or the other party. These reasons and some others like them did not greatly stir the patriotism of the women. A few women formed the League of Women Voters, a nonpartisan organization which tries, as far as human agencies can do so, to control the prejudices of its members and have them look at both sides of political questions and to furnish unbiased information to any women asking to know about candidates or measures proposed by any political party. Other organizations sprang up for political study and long established women's clubs added departments of citizenship where their politically minded members could study such questions as interested them.

❋ ❋ ❋

Some women have been educating themselves in the past fourteen years; the mass of their sisters is now awake. Are there women ready to lead in these new paths? Will other women follow them? We do not know, but one thing is sure, the attitude of women toward changes in society is going to determine to a great extent our future in this country. Women in the past have never realized their political strength. Will they wake up to it now? Will they realize that politics in the old sense, a game played for selfish ends by a few politicians, is of no concern any longer to any one and that recognition in the sense of receiving a political job is perhaps necessary but only important because of the opportunity it affords a woman or a man to show what they conceive to be the duty of a government servant? If our government offices are not held in the next few years by men and women with new conceptions of public service, then our revolution may not continue to be bloodless and changes may not come gradually as they are coming now, but violently and suddenly as they have come in the past in France and in Russia and we will go back before we gather up the pieces and move forward again.

So in reviewing the past fourteen years let us acknowledge that women have made a few changes in politics. It is quite safe for them to be at polling places on election day and very gradually the men are accepting them as part of the party machinery and to-day if a woman wants to work and can prove her ability and is not too anxious and insistent upon recognition and tangible reward, she can be part of almost any party activity except the inner circle where the really important decisions in city, county and state politics are made! She can get into this inner circle in national politics more easily than in state, county and city and I wonder if the reason might be that men in Washington are a little more formal with each other and therefore the presence of a woman does not "cramp their style" to the same degree that it would in the other conferences? Women have made no great changes in politics or government and that is all that can be said of the past and now for the present.

Women are thinking and that is the first step toward an increased and more intelligent use of the ballot. Then they will demand of their political parties clear statements of principles and they will scrutinize their party's candidates, watch their records, listen to their promises and expect them to live up to them and to have their party's backing, and occasionally when the need arises, women will reject their party and its candidates. This will not be disloyalty but will show that as members of a party they are loyal first to the fine things for which the party stands and when it rejects those things or forgets the legitimate objects for which political parties exist, then as a party it cannot command the honest loyalty of its members.

Next, I believe women will run for office and accept victory or defeat in a sporting spirit. The proportion of women holding elective office is small. There are two reasons for this: one is that many women have dreaded the give and take of a campaign, they have dreaded the public criticism, they have not learned to discount the attacks of the opposition; but business and professional life is paving the way and this reason will not deter them much longer.

The second reason is that as a rule nominations which are given women by any of the political parties are in districts where it is almost impossible for one holding their political beliefs to win; in other words, a woman who is willing to make a well-nigh hopeless fight is welcomed by a local leader trying to fill out his ticket. The changing attitude towards women in general may bring a change in this. We have good women in political office today and much depends on their success. They are blazing the new paths and what is far more important they are exemplifying what we mean by the new type of public servant. When Frances Perkins says, "I can't go away because under the new industrial bill we have a chance to achieve for the workers of this country better conditions for which I have worked all my life," she is not staying because she will gain anything materially, for herself or her friends, but because she sees an opportunity for government to render a permanent service to the general happiness of the working man and woman and their families. This is what we mean as I see it by the "new deal." Look carefully, O people, at the record of some of your public servants in the past few years! Does this attitude strike you as new? If so, the women are in part responsible for it, and I think at present we can count on a more active interest from them and a constantly increasing willingness to bear their proper share of the burdens of government.

Now for the dreams of the future:

If women are really going to awake to their civic duties, if they are going to accept changes in social living and try to make of this country a real democracy, in which the best of opportunity is available to every child and where the compensations of life are not purely material ones, then we may indeed be seeing the realization of a really new deal for the people. If this is to come true, it seems to be that the women have got to learn to work together even before they work with men, and they have got to be realistic in facing the social problems that have to be solved. They cannot accept certain doctrines simply because they sound well. I have often thought that it sounded so well to talk about women being on an equal footing with men and sometimes when I have listened to the arguments of the National Woman's Party and they have complained that they could not compete in the labor market because restrictions were laid upon women's work which were not laid upon men's, I have been almost inclined to agree with them that such restrictions were unjust, until I came to realize that when all is said and done, women *are* different from men. They are equals in many ways, but they cannot refuse to acknowledge their differences. Not to acknowledge them weakens the case. Their physical functions in life are different and perhaps in the same way the contributions which they are to bring to the spiritual side of life are different. It may be that certain questions are waiting to be solved until women can bring their views to bear upon those questions.

AN ESSAY ON WOMEN IN THE POST–WORLD WAR II PEACE SETTLEMENT, WRITTEN IN 1944

ER had pressured FDR and New Deal leaders to give women places of authority in government and during World War II in the war effort. Toward the end of that great world trauma, as FDR prepared to seek a fourth term in office, she began her own effort to have women play major roles in the peace settlement. In the April 1944 issue of the popular *Reader's Digest* she wrote the following manifesto for women:

No peace conference seems to be confronting us at the moment, but when and if there is one, I am confident that we will see women not only in the United States delegation but also from other countries. The interests of women who are fighting this war alongside the men cannot be ignored in any decisions for the future.

Through the years men have made the wars; it is only fair to suggest that women can help to make a lasting peace. Women are, because of their natural functions, the great conservers of life; men spend it. Men are now giving up, though rather reluctantly, their ancient prerogatives of deciding, without feminine assistance, the great questions of public policy.

Queen Elizabeth, Mrs. Winston Churchill, Lady Reading and many other British women stand out today as having prepared themselves during the war to face the problems of the postwar world. Certainly Queen Wilhelmina and Princess Juliana have been doing the same. From Madame Molotoff down, every woman in Russia has been taking her part in assisting the armed services.

Madame Chiang Kai-shek is never far away from her husband's side. In every country there are women ready to think in terms of postwar developments on a world scale.

As each future conference of the nations meets, women should be among the delegates, no matter what the subject under discussion. This is not only a question of the recognition of women, it is a question of education for citizenship.

If women do not sit side by side with men and hear the arguments as they develop, decisions will be made without the proper basis of knowledge, decisions which cannot be carried out unless the majority of the women in every country cooperate in making them successful. News travels fast through women's clubs; such organizations would help greatly in spreading information if some of their members sat in important councils with men.

I was proud that our nation had women present at the Food Conference, and was glad that on our delegation at the United Nations Relief and Rehabilitation Conference we had not only women delegates but several women as observers. The observers were women with interests in special fields; they brought up points that otherwise would not have been given adequate consideration. I hope that, as more conferences are called, we will see an increasing number of women take their places with men.

All nations are ruled primarily by self-interest, and women are not going to be different from men in that respect. But the men often think that our self-interest lies in reaching out for more power through force or through trade. Isn't it conceivable that women may think our self-interest lies in giving all the world a chance to envision something a little better than has been known before? That conception does not exist because women are more unselfish; it is because women value the conservation of human life more highly than the acquisition of power. Women will try to find ways to cooperate where men think only of dominating.

You will say that my thesis cannot be proved—and I will agree with you. Yet in the past, whenever women have shared in the councils of the mighty, there have been shining examples among them. Queen Elizabeth and Queen Victoria gave their country good leadership. Queen Wilhelmina is doing so today.

I can remember when women first began to be a factor in politics in this country, when it was generally said that "politics is no place for women." Men took off their coats and smoked big black cigars and put their feet on the tables and drank liquor and insisted that their political gatherings would offend the ladies. (The ladies seem to be surviving, however!)

Perhaps women haven't accomplished all they might have in politics, but there is a good deal more social legislation than there ever was before women had the vote. When a question comes up which really arouses the women of this country, believe me, the men know that women are now a real factor in politics.

My plea is not for women at a peace conference only. It is for women in every meeting which deals with postwar problems; more women among our state legislators, in our city governments; more women in Congress; more women in high appointive positions of responsibility. They will not be there to oppose men, but to work with men, to have a share in shaping the new world which, whether we want it or not, is going to confront us some day. Men and women will have to live in this new world together They should begin now to build it together.

An Essay, "Women Have Come a Long Way," Written in 1950, Five Years after Leaving the White House

In *It's up to the Women*, ER had entertained the question of whether there would ever be a woman President of the United States. She allowed that there would eventually be one, when the time came that a particular woman was prepared for such a heavy burden; but she conceded that this would probably not be in her own lifetime. As far as she could see, Presidents would be men.

In 1950, after she had been First Lady for twelve years and then a delegate to the United Nations for four more, she wrote the following essay for *Harper's* magazine. Times had changed. Women had served with efficiency and distinction in efforts to end the Depression and win the war. And she as much as any other person had been the agent of change. This is the way she felt about women and their public role as she entered the latter years of her life:

> As I look back over a rather long life I am impressed with the great changes that I have witnessed in the status of women. I was brought up by my grandmother from the time I was eight years old, so perhaps I see the differences in a somewhat more exaggerated form than some of my contemporaries who were never

under the direct influence of a member of that earlier generation. To my grandmother it was unthinkable that a girl should go to work unless she was destitute or at least really impoverished; and that she should wish to go to college seemed preposterous. But I imagine that most women who were brought up at the time I was, and in roughly the same sort of surroundings, will share my sense of the contrasts that have come about.

I learned to ride horseback, but I rode sidesaddle. I can remember the excitement there was over girls who rode bicycles wearing bloomers, and how outrageous many people thought them. We went bathing in bathing-suits with skirts, and long black stockings; propriety demanded that we be completely covered. And some girls even wore hats in bathing to shield them from the sun, for it was considered important to preserve the whiteness of one's skin: young ladies would have been dismayed at getting the healthy look of a tan that today they deliberately acquire in the South in the winter, and wherever they are in the summer.

At eighteen I was introduced to New York Society. I was a frightened young girl who had spent three years at a finishing school in Europe and had practically no friends, either male or female, in this country. There was still a Four Hundred in New York Society. If you belonged you were asked to the "right parties" and if you didn't belong you were not asked. In those days it took not only money but a really concentrated campaign to get recognition if you came as an unknown to New York. I remember a few lovely girls who took the city by storm, arriving from other parts of the country, but either they were great beauties or had a reputation for having brains and knew some of the "right" people to introduce them. People were just beginning to accept the fact that a Miss Livingston could marry a Mr. Mills from California; but on the whole New York Society was compact and chary of outsiders.

It was conceded that girls of Society families had an obligation to do some kind of charitable work, but very, very few of them took money-earning jobs: and if they "had to work," as the phrase of the day went, they were largely limited to becoming teachers, trained nurses, social workers, or librarians. Miss Elizabeth Marbury[1] once told me how horrified the New York Society of her young days was when she had to go to work and began to represent artists and build a talent office. A girl whose family was on a lower income level could be a clerk in a store or work in an office, but generally speaking she did this only so long as it was an abso-

---

[1] A talent agent and friend of Eleanor.

lute economic necessity; male pride and general public opinion frowned on any woman who worked outside the home if she could manage to avoid it. Not many executive positions were held by women and they had hardly begun to be recognized in the professions. That has come only after a long, hard fight; and few young things today have any idea of what they owe to the women who pioneered in higher education and in working in the professional fields.

We still heard with amusement and horror in the early nineteen-hundreds of the early fighters for suffrage who had worn trousers and walked around the streets of New York in them. Women were doing a great many things for the first time, but most of them were content to be housekeepers and mothers who stayed in the home—where they often worked very hard indeed—and many became pretty Society butterflies, spoiled and ruled by their husbands.

A change came with World War I. For large numbers of women who had to go to work when their husbands were in the service found they liked the new freedom and continued in their jobs after the war was over; the percentage of women working for wages outside the home jumped upward.

My mother had been well educated for a girl of her generation and she took a great interest in my education, but in those days a solid foundation of learning and training in the ability to think were less highly regarded than the social graces which made you attractive and charming in Society. I learned to speak French fluently before I learned to speak English, but my arithmetic was learned by rote without the slightest understanding of why certain things produced certain answers. I learned the whole of the first four books of Euclid by heart, and I have never understood what use that was in preparation for the life that I was expected to live in the future. Of course, I have had quite a different life from the one that my mother and grandmother envisioned for me; I was certainly not consciously prepared for it.

I was fifteen when I came in contact, in Europe, with the first women I had ever known who were really intellectually emancipated, and I found this experience extremely stimulating. The Boer War[2] was being fought and the Dreyfus[3] case was still being

---

[2] The war over control of South Africa between British and Dutch.
[3] Alfred Dreyfus, a French Jewish military officer, was convicted of treason, but later exonerated. The Dreyfus affair demonstrated the anti-Semitism prevalent even in nations like France.

argued. I heard the rights and wrongs of such public issues discussed at length and heatedly, in fact with passion—something
I had never heard at home. In my grandmother's home politics
were never mentioned and I think she was rather ashamed to
acknowledge that even by marriage anything so contaminating
as a government official was related to the family.

But if I was not brought up to be useful or to think of the
obligations to society that must be recognized by a conscientious
citizen of a democracy, I was nevertheless given a very free rein in
my intellectual development along many lines. The library in our
country house, as in the city house we lived in, was filled with
books gathered by my grandfather, who had had a special bent
toward theology, though apparently he never had any inclination
to become a minister. I never wanted to read the books on theology (though I remember shedding tears over the illustrations in
the Doré Bible[4]); but other books on those shelves—the classics,
biographies, travel, novels, stories about life anywhere of any
kind—fed the interests of my childhood and helped to show me,
eventually, why so many women were beginning to fight for
equality in the political and social world which up to that time
had seemed of very little importance to me.

I had my first contact with the suffrage movement rather late,
and consider myself lucky to have heard Anna Howard Shaw
speak and to have known Carrie Chapman Catt[5] before she was
widely recognized as the great leader of women in the struggle
for equal political rights.

As a result of the shift of public opinion which these women
helped to bring about, there have been far-reaching amendments
during the past fifty years of the laws which touch on the rights of
women. These vary in different parts of the world and, for that
matter, in different states in our own country. The old Blue Laws[6]
which were accepted throughout New England at one time may
still be on the statute books, but even where such antiquated legislation remains it is completely ignored, and by and large women
seem to be considered as equals before the law in the United
States. Of late there has been a great agitation to pass an equal
rights amendment; but I think that if one looks over the reforms
of the past generation one must decide that it would be easier in

---

[4] The "Doré Bible was illustrated by French graphic artist Paul-Gustave Doré.

[5] Shaw and Catt were suffragists, fighters for women's right to vote.

[6] Laws designed to enforce morals, particularly regarding the observance of Sunday as the Christian day of rest.

our particular situation to change such state laws as seem to discriminate against women than to pass a federal amendment.

Women have now become an integral part of nearly all the
trade unions, and it is interesting to note that some of the unions
in the industries which employ largely women are as good as any
there are.

In family life, too, the change has been great. Fifty years ago
women had to resort to subtlety if they wished to exert influence;
now their influence is exerted openly and accepted by husband
and children. Fifty years ago no young girl had an apartment of
her own while she was single; "Mrs. Grundy"[7] frowned on that.
Today no one questions the right of an adult woman to have her
own home.

In my lifetime I have seen women accepted as doctors, sur-
geons, psychiatrists, lawyers, architects, and even, during the war,
as mechanics on the assembly line. I remember the day when
John Golden[8] said in the White House that women lacked the
power to be creative and that there had never been any great
creative women artists. I took that up seriously with him later, and
contended that this might seem to be true in our time, but had
not always been true in the past: and that if it was true, this was
not because women lacked ability but because they lacked opportunity. I think that today we must realize that in the past generation we have developed many very able writers and painters and
some very able sculptors among the women of this country and
other countries. Modern life moves very quickly and the distrac-
tions and multitudinous occupations that are thrust upon women
tend to make the development of an artist's creative talents more
difficult than in the past; but in spite of these outward circumstances the urge to create is so strong that I think we are going
to find more and more women expressing themselves not only
through the bearing and rearing of children but through the creative arts.

One thing that strikes me particularly today is the way in which
women are accepting responsibility in creating the pattern for the
new states. Take India, for example. I have seen in the United
Nations a woman delegate, Madame Pandit, the sister of the
Prime Minister, lead her delegation—the only woman to occupy
such a position.

---

[7] A term used to describe a conservative, older woman.
[8] John Golden was a theatrical producer and close friend both of ER and FDR. She
obviously felt that she could speak to him frankly.

ER with a group representing three of her main causes: women, youth, and support of the United Nations

I have been impressed, too, with the number of women of charm and ability who have come to the United Nations with good backgrounds of work in various fields that fit them for their duties in that body. I think at once of Madame Lefoucheaux of France, who was chairman of the last meeting of the Commission on the Status of Women; Miss Bowie, who represented the United Kingdom on the Human Rights Commission; Madame Hansa Mehta of India, also on this commission; and many women who have acted as advisers to the harried delegates and brought us the information without which some of us would have found it very difficult to carry on the work confronting us in fields in which we had had little or no experience. Even ten years ago, if there had been such a body as the United Nations, it would hardly have been possible to find women sitting as delegates, and certainly it would have been considered doubtful whether the United States would ever send a woman as a delegate. Now it sends a woman alternate as well!

Perhaps the position of women in the United Nations is the best example of the fact that they have graduated from exclusion

from business and the professions to almost complete acceptance and equality, and that they are now generally treated as
virtually on a par with men in the political world at home and
abroad. Some nations are slower in granting this recognition
than others, but the trend is unmistakable. It is toward complete
equality.

I think it might still be said that if a woman wants really to succeed she must do better than a man, for she is under more careful
scrutiny; but this is practically the only handicap under which
women now labor in almost any field of endeavor.

THE FINAL CRUSADE: ER AS CHAIR OF THE KENNEDY COMMISSION ON THE STATUS OF WOMEN

Through the 1950s, although she held no official position in the
government, ER continued to work for the rights and advancement
of women. She twice supported the presidential candidacy of
Adlai Stevenson (1952 and 1956) and was twice disappointed that
the liberal Democrat lost to war hero Dwight D. Eisenhower. As
the 1960 election approached she once again favored Stevenson
and was leery of John Kennedy. She remembered his father Joseph,
a rival of FDR, and she suspected Kennedy's commitment to racial
justice and women's rights. Only after he was the Democratic nominee and came to seek her support did she give him her endorsement, saying he seemed ready to learn his job.

Kennedy, elected by a razor-thin margin, had no strong cre-
dentials on women's issues. He appointed Esther Peterson director of the Women's Bureau of the Department of Labor and gave
her instructions to study the issue of women in American society.
Peterson opposed the adoption of an Equal Rights Amendment to
the U.S. Constitution for much the same reason ER had opposed
it, that it would make women seem a separate class, believing that
if existing rights were guaranteed women would be equal. She
created, in December 1961, the President's Commission on the
Status of Women—and named ER its chair.

The story of ER's brief but decisive tenure as chair of the
"Kennedy Commission," which ended when her health failed in
1962, is told by Professor Lois Sharf, author of among other books
The Women's Movement, 1920–1940:

Roosevelt brought her usual organizational skills and commitments to the commission, but they were not really necessary. From limited space in Peterson's Labor Department base and with no appropriation until the following fiscal year, she directed all functions. The commission divided its proposed survey into seven areas: federal employment, government contracts and private employment, federal taxes and social security, services for home and community, education, protective labor legislation, and civil and political rights. The last area—civil and political rights—was the one directly concerned with the Equal Rights Amendment, although the issue lay at the core of the entire undertaking.

At the first sessions of the commission in February 1962, which Roosevelt hosted at Hyde Park, she proved a safe choice as Peterson's carefully selected honorary chair. A member who represented the Council of Jewish Women voiced the feeling of her constituents that the commission was organized in order to promote the constitutional amendment. Eleanor replied simply, "It is odd, because for many years I opposed the equal rights of women." By refusing to make it clear that she had ceased to challenge the amendment, she perpetuated the notion that her opposition remained unchanged.

Following the February meetings, Eleanor Roosevelt became ill. Except for a late-fall TV appearance on "Issues and Answers" with Esther Peterson, her first and only chairing of those sessions marked her last public role. After ER's death in November 1962, Peterson wrote to member Margaret Hickey that everyone involved should "carry out the policies Mrs. Roosevelt initiated, and . . . strive to make the work of this Commission not only a memorial to its late chairman, but a fitting and appropriate reflection of the incomparable service she performed in a lifetime of devotion to the public good." Peterson assumed real as well as apparent control. In 1963 the commission's final report, *American Women,* downgraded discriminatory practices that still hampered women and presented an optimistic picture of women fulfilling their traditional, primary roles in the home and, increasingly, new roles in the workplace, where they represented a potential resource for strengthening the nation. The longer reports of the Committees on Protective Legislation and on Political Civil Rights concluded that protective legislation was still needed, and "a constitutional amendment need not now be sought in order to establish this principle [of equality of rights for men and women]." The report not only reiterated the views that Peterson articulated in 1960 to the Democratic platform committee, but only slightly went beyond perspectives on female status then forty years old.

Although Eleanor Roosevelt did not live to complete her task of chairing the commission, the reports provide a vantage point from which to assess her feminism. As early as 1935, Ruby Black had excused ER from the ultimate litmus test of the National Woman's Party: she did not have to back the ERA to qualify as a feminist, as long as she was conscious of the liabilities in the paths of women, articulated women's concerns over those discriminations clearly, and promoted the status of qualified women in government and the professions. But Black added personal autonomy and self-definition to more conventional concepts of public positions and actions. Roosevelt qualified as a feminist, according to Black, because she lived like a feminist—working and earning her own income, achieving a measure of economic independence, and believing that women should be recognized in their own right and not as reflections of husbands and fathers.

TWO ASSESSMENTS OF ELEANOR ROOSEVELT'S WORK FOR WOMEN'S RIGHTS: JOSEPH LASH AND SUSAN HARTMANN

Joseph Lash, a young man who came to know ER during her years in the White House, had an opportunity to observe the work she did to advance women firsthand. The following selection, from his book *Eleanor and Franklin*, recounts the achievements of her earliest days in the White House:

There was another sign of her intense practicality—the way she backed up her exhortations to women to take leadership in the fight against war and social injustice with hard-headed political organization. Many women held important positions in the Roosevelt administration, she noted in *It's up to the Women*, and were, therefore, in a stronger position to shape policy than ever before. The book did not say what insiders in Washington knew, that at the center of this growing New Deal political sisterhood was Eleanor Roosevelt.

"About the most important letter I ever wrote you!" Molly Dewson[9] scribbled on the margin of a seven-page enclosure she

---

[9] Molly Dewson headed the Women's Division of the Democratic National Committee. She later served in the Social Security Administration.

sent Mrs. Roosevelt a few weeks after the Roosevelts arrived in Washington. The letter reported on Molly's talk with James Farley, the postmaster general, about women's patronage. He would make no appointments of women, Farley assured Molly, without consulting Eleanor, so Molly felt safe about the lists she had left with him, which described the jobs the Democratic women wanted in categories of descending urgency. "Imperative recognition" covered the four appointments to the staff of the Democratic National Committee, followed by the names of fourteen women who warranted "Very Important Recognition" and twenty-five for whom jobs were sought under the classification of "Very Desirable Recognition." Postmasterships and comparable minor appointments were listed under the heading of "Worthy of Lesser Recognition."

"I think they are '100 percent' friendly toward recognizing the work of the Women and that they will probably do it," Molly's letter continued. But she cautioned Eleanor that the men were lobbying for jobs so insistently "that continuous pressure will have to be brought on Mr. Farley on behalf of the women. I mean continuous in the sense of pressure on behalf of one woman today and another woman tomorrow."

Mrs. Roosevelt and Molly Dewson were determined that women's voices should be heard at every level of the new administration, and they worked as a team to bring this about, although as far as the world knew Molly was the chief dispenser of the New Deal's feminine patronage. The relationship between Eleanor and Molly was harmonious and sympathetic. They had a common conception of the importance of building party organization and of using the influence of women to achieve the objectives of the New Deal.

Eleanor persuaded Farley to make the women's division a full-time functioning department of the Democratic National Committee, and then she and the president prevailed upon Molly Dewson to come to Washington to head the department. On January 15, 1934, despite her ban on political subjects, Eleanor presented Molly at her press conference to describe the new setup of the women's Democratic organization. When Molly said that women Democrats had long hoped for such an organization and were now about to achieve it "for many reasons," Ruby Black of the United Press, who knew Mrs. Roosevelt's decisive role behind the scenes, mischievously blurted out, "name three." Eleanor gave her a humorously reproving glance, and Molly, after a pause, said, "This Democratic party really believes in women, and the plan was presented to it properly." Molly arrived in the capital with the names of sixty women qualified on the basis of their work in the campaign and their past records to hold high government positions. By April, 1935, the Associated Press reported that there were more than fifty women in such positions, and many of them made public pronouncements under Eleanor's auspices. Secretary of Labor Frances W. Perkins announced the establishment of camps for unemployed women at one of Eleanor's press conferences. It was in Eleanor's sitting room that Mrs. Mary Harriman Rumsey, the chairman of the NRA Consumer's Advisory Board, described her group's efforts to combat rising prices through local consumer organization. And the plans of the Civil Works Administration to provide 100,000 jobs for women were first disclosed by the new director of the CWA's women's work, Mrs. Ellen S. Woodward, at a joint press conference with the First Lady.

"I do happen to know, from my close connections with the business and professional women, of the resentment felt against Hoover because he did not recognize women," Judge Florence E. Allen of the Ohio supreme court wrote Eleanor in expressing her pleasure in the new administration's appointment of women. Such recognition did not come automatically—not even in the New Deal. Molly fought vigorously to enlarge the number of positions open to women. Sometimes she won her point on her own, but if not, she went to Eleanor, and Eleanor, if she ran into difficulty, turned to Louis or Franklin. Occasionally nothing worked. When Secretary of State Hull recommended the appointment of Lucile Foster McMillin to the place on the Civil Service Commission that traditionally had gone to a woman, Molly complained to Eleanor, "Don't you really think that Secretary Hull has enough recognition and power in his own job not to take away from the regular organization women the few jobs that have always been marked out for them?" Why didn't he appoint Mrs. McMillin to a diplomatic post? But then, she added apologetically, "Of course, I realize I may be asking more from you than is possible at this stage of woman's development." Hull had his way and Mrs. McMillin was named Civil Service commissioner, but several years later he did name two women as American ministers—"the first time in our history that women had been named to head diplomatic missions," he would proudly write, adding with male condescension, "They both proved competent, and made excellent records."

Harry Hopkins was much more receptive to the wishes of the women, especially Eleanor. He was as passionate a reformer as she and just as ready for bold experimentation. He cultivated her interest in the Civil Works Administration and encouraged her to take the lead in setting up the women's end of the CWA. "You may be sure that under the new Civil Works program women will not be overlooked," Eleanor assured a woman correspondent who was upset that the president's announcement of the CWA omitted specific mention of women. A program for unemployed women was hammered out at a White House conference called and key-noted by Eleanor and attended by the leading figures in the field of social welfare. By the end of 1933, 100,000 women had CWA jobs.

The irascible and aggressive Harold L. Ickes was touchier to deal with. When Eleanor went to him with a request, she was usually careful to preface it with the statement that the president had asked her to do so. This was the case when she urged that the post of assistant commissioner of education, "which is now held by a woman [should] be retained by a woman" and that under the plan to provide work for unemployed teachers, half the positions should be allotted to women. Ickes agreed on both points.

While she sought through patronage to build up the women's division of the party, Eleanor insisted that appointments had to be on the basis of merit, not just party loyalty, particularly as she felt that "during the next few years, at least, every woman in public office will be watched far more carefully than a man holding a similar position." Farley, under pressure from a female party worker for one of the top jobs in the administration, turned to Eleanor, who noted that "as head of the Children's Bureau, she [the woman in question] would be appalling. . . . I imagine she is entitled to something if it can be had and I also imagine that she needs the money badly, but I would not sacrifice a good job for her."

While pressing for the appointment of Democratic women, Eleanor would not agree to the removal of outstanding women who happened to be Republicans. The head of the Children's Bureau, Grace Abbott, a Republican, had been one of the three top-ranking women in Washington under Hoover. Although she militantly championed children's rights, ambitious Democrats tried to use Miss Abbott's party affiliation as an excuse for Farley to force her out. Eleanor advised Farley to write the woman who was after Dr. Abbott's job "that no change is being made in the Children's Bureau and that Miss Abbott has the backing of most of the organized groups of women interested in child welfare."

Although she wanted the Democrats to become the majority party, which it was not in 1932, Eleanor did not hesitate to urge women to be ready to reject the party and its candidates "when the need arises."

> This will not be disloyalty but will show that as members of a party they are loyal first to the fine things for which the party stands and when it rejects those things or forgets the legitimate objects for which parties exist, then as a party it cannot command the honest loyalty of its members.

Basically what she hoped might result from the inclusion of women was a humanization of government services and programs.

At a dinner honoring the new secretary of labor, Eleanor stressed that the post had been given to Frances Perkins "not only because there was a demand on the part of the women that a woman should be given a place in the Cabinet, but because the particular place which she occupies could be better filled by her than by anyone else, man or woman, with whom the President was acquainted." But beyond that, Miss Perkins exemplified the new type of public servant who was being brought to Washington by the New Deal.

> When Frances Perkins says "I can't go away because under the new industrial bill (NIRA) we have a chance to achieve for the workers of this country better conditions for which I have worked all my life," she is not staying because she will gain anything materially for herself or her friends, but because she sees an opportunity for government to render a permanent service to the general happiness of the working man and woman and their families. This is what we mean as I see it by the "new deal."

If this attitude toward public service struck people as new, "the women are in part responsible for it."

Louis Howe, who shared Eleanor's view that women were in the forefront of the revolution in thinking that was back of the New Deal, believed that revolution would soon make it possible to elect a woman president. "If the women progress in their knowledge and ability to handle practical political and governmental questions with the same increasing speed as they have during the last ten years, within the next decade, not only the possibility but the advisability of electing a woman as President of the United States will become a seriously argued question," he wrote, adding that if politics continued to divide along humanitarian-conservative lines and the people decided they wanted a New Deal approach to such issues as education, recreation, and labor, "it is not without the bounds of possibility that a woman might not only be nominated but elected to that office on the grounds that they better understand such questions than the men."

Louis was so persuaded that the country might in the not-too-distant future say "Let's try a woman" that one day he came into Eleanor's sitting room, propped himself cross-legged on a daybed, and said, "Eleanor, if you want to be President in 1940, tell me now so I can start getting things ready." One politician in the family was enough, was her reply to such proposals, seriously meant or not. She did not deceive herself about the real attitude of the country, and doubted that the election of a woman was as imminent as Louis thought. "I do not think it would be impossible to find a woman who could be President, but I hope that it doesn't happen in the near future. . . . I do not think we have yet reached the point where the majority of our people would feel satisfied to follow the leadership and trust the judgment of a woman as President." Some day it might come to pass "but I hope it will not be while we speak of a 'woman's vote.' I hope it only becomes a reality when she is elected as an individual, because of her capacity and the trust which a majority of the people have in her integrity and ability as a person."

Women would have to learn that no amount of masculine chivalry was going to give them leadership if they could not actually "deliver the goods." They should leave their "womanly personalities" at home and "disabuse their male competitors of the old idea that women are only 'ladies in business.'" Women must stand or fall "on their own ability, on their own characters as persons. Insincerity and sham, whether in men or in women, always fail in the end in public life."

Professor Susan Hartmann of Ohio State University, who represents women more than a generation younger than ER, takes up Lash's story and carries her work in behalf of women through the remainder of her career. This selection is taken from the book *Eleanor Roosevelt: An American Journey:*

Eleanor Roosevelt's relationship to the struggle for women's equality was so complex that historians continue to differ over whether or not to characterize her as a feminist. On the one hand, Roosevelt was absent from the ranks of those campaigning for woman's suffrage in the 1910s and she publicly opposed the

Equal Rights Amendment[10] until the 1950s. Not infrequently, she articulated traditional attitudes about women, indicating acceptance of their secondary and subordinate roles in relationship to men. But her most active years in public life coincided with the period between 1920 and 1960, when feminist activism had declined after the suffrage victory, not to emerge as a major force in American life until the 1960s. Thus, any assessment of her feminism must take into account the constraints imposed by the climate of the times as well as by her position within the American establishment.

Roosevelt identified herself as a feminist. "I became a much more ardent citizen and feminist than anyone . . . would have dreamed possible," she wrote in the 1930s. A decade later she characterized herself as "an old woman who has worked on one front or another for almost forty-odd years for women's rights." Indeed, Eleanor Roosevelt was one of a relatively small group of women who formed a bridge between the suffrage movement and the contemporary feminist movement. Although she and most activist women opposed the Equal Rights Amendment, primarily because they believed that it would remove badly needed protections for employed women, they worked for women's rights in other ways. They achieved small but significant gains for women and even when success eluded them, they kept issues alive to be taken over by a later generation of feminists.

As First Lady, Roosevelt made unprecedented use of her position both to advance women as individuals and to focus attention on issues which concerned them. Through her energetic participation in public affairs she herself served as a role model and source of encouragement for women; but she also used her access to Administration and Democratic party officials to get women appointed to federal and state offices and to increase their presence and influence within the party. At the same time Roosevelt imparted visibility and legitimacy to women's concerns in her press conferences, speeches and public statements, and by hosting White House conferences which dealt with women's issues.

Roosevelt's press conferences illustrate how these two strategies worked together. Taking advantage of the media's interest in

---

[10] Proposed during the 1930s, the E.R.A. passed Congress in 1972, only to fail by 1982 to be ratified by three-fourths of the states. ER feared such an amendment might undermine laws protecting women. She reluctantly supported it before her death.

her, she used meetings with reporters to speak out on women's issues, and she invited other women leaders to speak at her press conferences. In addition, these meetings with reporters were open to women only. Thus, Roosevelt made it necessary for newspapers to employ women reporters if they were to have access to the First Lady.

The causes which Roosevelt promoted on behalf of women throughout her public career were numerous and varied. She defended married women's right to independence under the law and promoted women's equal access to jury service when a majority of states continued to deny women that fundamental exercise of citizenship. Roosevelt supported birth control when it was still encumbered by legal restrictions, and she assisted groups promoting the use of federal funds for family planning services. During World War II she pressed for women's opportunity to volunteer for military service on an equal basis with men and specifically urged the military to commission women doctors in the medical corps.

Three areas demand particular attention in any assessment of Eleanor Roosevelt's efforts to improve women's status and opportunities. Roosevelt demonstrated an especially deep and vigorous commitment to enlarging women's economic security and opportunity, to increasing their representation as appointed and elected officials, and to alleviating the particular problems faced by black women.

Particularly in the early years of the New Deal, during the darkest days of the Great Depression, Roosevelt devoted considerable attention to the impoverishment of women. In so doing, she took on a constant struggle against popular and official assumptions that since men were "breadwinners," they were the appropriate targets of relief and recovery programs. One of her earliest acts as First Lady was to convene a White House Conference on Emergency Needs for Women, a meeting in which women demonstrated that they too were breadwinners and suffered from unemployment and poverty. Roosevelt, along with women officials whom she had helped bring into New Deal agencies, persistently pressed relief officials to provide jobs for women in the public works programs. She criticized the tendency of public and private employers to discriminate against married women on the assumption that they did not need jobs. And she spoke out against the practice of paying women less than men on work relief projects. In the 1940s she supported federal equal pay legislation, and one of her last public activities was her testimony in 1962 to a Congressional committee considering an equal pay bill. That goal, which Roosevelt and other women had kept alive for two decades, became law in 1963 and served as a spur to the emerging women's movement of the 1960s.

Although women's issues claimed less of her attention in the 1940s, Roosevelt continued to speak out on issues concerning women's economic status and opportunities. During World War II she entreated employers to hire women in defense industries and insisted that women workers not be shunted aside after the war. As the wartime emergency brought millions more women into the labor force and as married women increasingly took jobs outside the home, Roosevelt focused attention on the double burden of women who combined paid work with their traditional family responsibilities. She urged shopkeepers to stay open in the evening, she promoted the use of federal funds to establish day care centers for the children of employed mothers and she sought continued state support for day care after the war. Although Roosevelt did not challenge the traditional assumption that women were responsible for child care and housework, she did publicize the difficulties encountered by women who added work outside the home to their customary household duties and suggested ways of easing this for women. This too became an issue of great importance to the contemporary feminist movement.

A second, and perhaps even more important area of concern to Roosevelt, was the need to get women into positions of political power. She fully understood the difficulties this entailed. In a private remark about problems Frances Perkins was encountering as secretary of labor, Roosevelt commented, "How men hate a woman in a position of real power." Later, she described her own situation as a member of the United States delegation to the United Nations: "I knew that as the only woman in the delegation I was not very welcome." Roosevelt also realized the burden of responsibility to other women that was placed upon women in exceptional positions. But she welcomed the responsibility to open doors for other women and encouraged other women leaders to do the same. Roosevelt believed that women in politics had to start at the bottom and "learn their jobs in public life step by step," but to her the most important thing for women to learn was "to take other women with them."

Women made larger gains in government and party positions in the 1930s than at any other time until the 1970s. The credit for this achievement belonged to Roosevelt and to Molly Dewson, head of the Democratic party's Women's Division, who relentlessly urged the appointment of women to political office. Roosevelt continued to work toward this goal for the rest of her life. When, during World War II, she said that "women should serve on all commissions that are an outgrowth of this global war" leaders of women's organizations took up this challenge and worked with the First Lady to implement it. In June 1944, she hosted a White House Conference on "How Women May Share in Post-War Policy-Making." Roosevelt gave the opening and closing remarks at the conference, and the two hundred women in attendance established a committee which composed a roster of women qualified for such posts. They presented the roster to the president and secretary of state and that presentation was announced at one of Eleanor Roosevelt's press conferences.

As she had done in the New Deal years, Roosevelt provided public visibility and a practical plan for getting women into positions of power. She did not relinquish this endeavor when she left the White House. After President John F. Kennedy had taken office, Roosevelt wrote him, noting that of his first 240 appointments only nine were women. She pointed out that women in other countries occupied more and higher positions than they did in the United States and she appended a three-page list of women qualified for government service.

Finally, Roosevelt channeled her concerns for women's rights and for civil rights into a specific focus on women who suffered from both racism and sexism. Mary McLeod Bethune[11] was one of the women appointed to New Deal agencies in part through the efforts of Roosevelt. Her relationship with Bethune went beyond friendship and support for Bethune as an individual to cooperation with her to address problems common to all black women. In 1938, Roosevelt sponsored a conference on the Participation of Negro Women and Children in Federal Programs. That meeting was the first major activity of the National Council of Negro Women which Bethune had founded in 1935. At the conference women representing nearly fifty organizations which were members of the council presented their views and recommendations to women in federal agencies. Roosevelt thus offered black women access to decision-makers and imparted legitimacy to their concerns.

---

[11] Bethune was a southern black woman educator who worked as Director of Minority Affairs for the New Deal's National Youth Administration. As such, she was a member of FDR's "Black Cabinet."

Roosevelt supported Bethune and the National Council of Negro Women even when to do so caused difficulties for her. She wrote in 1940, "I think I am going to get into trouble over a colored convention of women which Mrs. Bethune asked me to have. . . . It appears that they are mainly Republicans and the Democrats are annoyed." Roosevelt not only used her position to provide visibility and access to power for black women, but she also encouraged white women to combat racism. In the 1940s she promoted the establishment of a coalition of black and white women's organizations whose purpose was to work toward better race relations and she addressed the founding conference of the coalition.

Eleanor Roosevelt's last official appointment was as chair of Kennedy's Commission on the Status of Women. That position aptly symbolized the link Roosevelt formed between the older women's movement and the new feminism. The commission was first proposed in the 1940s and Eleanor Roosevelt was its most prominent advocate. In a most immediate way, the commission helped to launch the new feminism. By focusing attention on women's status, by documenting the existence of sex discrimination and raising expectations for its amelioration and by generating a network of women concerned about inequity, the commission helped to set off a movement which continues to strive for many of the hopes which Eleanor Roosevelt articulated for women from the 1920s to the 1960s.

A TRIBUTE FROM CONGRESSWOMAN ELEANOR HOLMES NORTON

Eleanor Holmes Norton, who serves in the 105th Congress as the District of Columbia's nonvoting delegate to the U.S. House of Representatives, represents in her person two of the groups Eleanor Roosevelt hoped to see advanced in American society: blacks and women. Representative Norton was in fact named for Eleanor Roosevelt because, she says, her father had such high hopes for her and because he admired Mrs. Roosevelt so much. "It was like being a child of the sixteenth century," she says, "and being named Elizabeth." In the following public address, with which she opened a centennial symposium on the life and work of Eleanor Roosevelt in 1984, she pays tribute to the woman who achieved so much for both black people and women:

Eleanor pursued the rights of both minorities and women because she understood that human rights is all or nothing. It is not like the severability clause lawyers put into contracts and statutes, that if one part is ruled invalid or inoperative the rest of the contract remains. Our contract is organic. Racism destroys it; sexism shreds it; anti-Semitism tears it apart. Prejudice based on ethnic origin, religion or similar characteristics demeans it.

In times like these we would do well to remember Eleanor's holistic view of human rights. In the face of a far right movement on the rise, we who cherish human rights must reassert the fundamental solidarity of all human beings. There needs to be much more forthright and outspoken leadership against the possibility of a schism between blacks and Jews. The common interests of workers of all backgrounds needs reaffirmation. We need greater clarity from the leadership of the civil rights and the women's rights movements that these two groups are in harmony, not in competition for affirmative action or anything else.

Eleanor instinctively understood this basic unity of purpose. She was in the great tradition of Americans who have dealt with human rights as whole cloth. Her antecedents included black Americans like Sojourner Truth and Frederick Douglass,[12] who joined their resolute abolitionism with a fervent feminism. On the question of the necessity of both race and sex equality, Sojourner Truth would brook no compromise. Indeed when the tricky question arose of whether the Fifteenth Amendment should be supported if it contained no enfranchisement of women she said that limiting the vote to men would mean that "men will be the masters over women, and it will be just as bad as it was before." Frederick Douglass never forgot that white women had been the first abolitionists and they in turn recognized him, in the words of one women's rights leader of the period, as "the most conspicuous advocate of our rights." Douglass remembered that in the 1830s and 1840s women had formed not women's rights groups but anti-slavery societies. Throughout his life Douglass spoke and acted as a dedicated feminist and called himself a "women's rights man." When the time came to change the name of his paper he refused to call it *The Brotherhood* because, he said, it "implied the exclusion of the sisterhood." The timeless tradition of Frederick Douglass and Sojourner Truth passed into Eleanor's life.

---

[12] Truth and Douglass were both former slaves, staunch abolitionists, and advocates for women's rights.

If we continue to draw from her life, our generation may yet be remembered more for its contribution to conceptions of justice and equality than for its role as pioneers of the space age. This generation's accomplishments—in the great civil rights legislation and in pathbreaking court decisions—are a truly national achievement. What has been achieved in America is a new majority for equality. And this majority continues to hold despite negative national leadership on equality and despite the emergence of organized reactionaries who yearn for simpler times.

As Americans pass through the unsettling transition that characterizes our time, we could do with large and daring figures like Eleanor. At this great moment of change on so many fundamental matters, we would do well to see ourselves as perhaps endowed with a special mission—a mission for our own generation. The generation of Americans that lived in the last quarter of the eighteenth century defined the character of our great governing institutions. Eleanor's generation that shaped the 1930s redefined the relationship between the individual and the state to include shared responsibility to relieve human suffering. My generation of black students from the 1960s, I believe it is fair to say, redefined what it means to be black in America, and because of the centrality of race in the American experience, partially redefined what it means to be American as well. Where is the vanguard of the leadership needed for this period in American life? Where are the Eleanors? Where is the leadership that must help replace what has fallen because of inequality or injustice or sheer inadequacy? Where is the leadership to rebuild an America undergoing vast changes in individual roles and institutional needs?

Without the wonderful props of Eleanor's times, without the highs and the lows, without the dramatic rhetoric, without the charismatic leaders, without the mass approval, with only the nation's best ideals, with a fresh and unscarred sense of the possible, with an often lonely sense of mission, with these and not much more, what has been begun must somehow be finished. If sometimes the national mood seems pointed to yesterday, Eleanor Roosevelt reminds us that "tomorrow is now." We pause to recall her life not only because it was so noble. We need her life to reinforce the march toward that day when, at long last, the dawn reveals the sunlit fields and the sturdy mountains of a nation where justice guards the night and rules the day.

After reviewing ER's life and achievements, no one can doubt that she made a deep and lasting impression on the United States and the world. In choosing to champion social, economic, racial, and international justice, she brought the power and influence of her name and position to bear on the most profound and complex of American and world problems. She made Americans aware not only of these problems but of their responsibility to solve them. Without question she is a Creator of the American mind.

QUESTIONS FOR RESPONSIVE ESSAYS

1. What was Eleanor Roosevelt's assessment of the place of women in American society when she entered the White House in 1933? How were her opinions molded by her experiences to that time? In what ways was she a woman of her time, and in what ways was she ahead of her time?

2. How did ER's assessment of the place of women change during her time as First Lady, as expressed in her essays of 1944 and 1950? How much of this change came because of her success in promoting women? Taking her philosophy and life's work as a whole, should ER be called a feminist?

3. How was ER's philosophy of social reform related to her work for women's rights? How was she able to combine her efforts on behalf of women with those for minorities and workers? In what ways was she consistent and in what ways inconsistent? How was she at times a woman of her age and at others a woman far ahead of her times?

4. How do the assessments of ER's work for women by Joseph Lash and Susan Hartmann agree and how do they differ? Does the male writer Lash see the woman's question differently from the female writer Hartmann? Using their points of agreement, what would you say were ER's assumptions, her policies, and her achievements in the field of women's rights?

5. How does the contemporary public figure Eleanor Holmes Norton evaluate the significance of ER for our times? Must we see her simply as a figure in history, or can we use our understanding of her work to apply her principles and policies to our own day with its particular problems and issues? How do you think ER would approach such issues as abortion, welfare, and affirmative action?

SUGGESTED TOPICS FOR ESSAYS OR PAPERS

1. "Eleanor Roosevelt and the Role of the First Lady in American Political History." This paper would be a survey of the way various First Ladies have responded to the demands of this unelected office, with particular emphasis on Eleanor Roosevelt and the way she changed the role. The paper could examine what personal traits and convictions ER brought to the White House that made her revolutionary. It might even ask whether the change she made has been a positive benefit to the nation.

2. "Eleanor Roosevelt and the New Deal." This paper would survey the achievements of FDR's New Deal programs and show how the First Lady contributed to the debates on those programs. Since no one questions the fact that the New Deal forever changed the way Americans thought of their government and its role in their lives, it would be enlightening to see just how much influence ER did or did not have in making the Roosevelt revolution.

3. "Eleanor Roosevelt and Twentieth-Century American Social Movements." Beginning with the Progressive movement of the early twentieth century, social movements leading to great changes have been characteristic of American politics. As a child of the Progressive movement (her Uncle Theodore was a Progressive President), ER's encouragement of minorities and women gave great strength to the Civil Rights movement of the 1950s an 1960s and the Feminist movement of the 1970s and 1980s. An examination of just how she influenced these movements would be exciting.

4. "Eleanor Roosevelt and the Issue of War and Peace." This paper might explore how and why ER changed from being a pacifist in the early days to being a strong supporter of the effort to defeat Germany and Japan in World War II. Interesting questions

could be examined: Was she ever a true pacifist? Was she more a pragmatic politician, supporting her husband's policies at the outbreak of war, than a true idealist? Did she believe that World War II was, in philosophical terms, "a just war"? What part did her love for England and France, which she developed as a young woman, play in the change of attitude? What did she contribute to the war effort, and how much difference did she actually make?

5. "Eleanor Roosevelt and the Post–World War II Peace." Here one might examine ER's role in the creation of the United Nations, particularly its humanitarian branch, and in writing the Universal Declaration of Human Rights. It is possible also to show her continuing influence, through the 1950s, as she spoke and wrote on racial, social, economic, and gender issues, culminating with her chairing the Kennedy Commission on the Status of Women.

ANNOTATED
BIBLIOGRAPHY

Books

Maurine Beasley. *Eleanor Roosevelt and the Media.* Urbana and Chicago: University of Illinois Press, 1987. This book shows how ER used the mass media to promote her causes. She not only held press conferences but also wrote columns and articles for popular audiences.

Jason Berger. *A New Deal for the World: Eleanor Roosevelt and American Foreign Policy.* New York: Columbia University Press, 1981. This book is helpful when studying ER's role in World War II and in the founding of the United Nations just after the war.

Allida Black. *Casting Her Own Shadow: Eleanor Roosevelt and the Shaping of Postwar Liberalism.* New York: Columbia University Press, 1996. Professor Black demonstrates the ways ER continued, on her own after 1945, to press for her causes: fair employment, civil rights for women and minorities, and world peace.

Blanche Wiesen Cook. *Eleanor Roosevelt.* New York: Viking Press, Volume One 1992, Volume Two 1998. This is the most complete recent biography of ER, using the latest research. Cook examines ER's career as woman, wife, mother, politician, and diplomat.

Helen Gahagan Douglas. *The Eleanor Roosevelt We Remember.* New York: Hill and Wang, 1963. Douglas, who was ER's personal friend and political ally, provides valuable insights about her personal and political style, along with one of the best collections of photographs of her from the various periods of her life.

Jess Flemion and Colleen O'Connor (eds). *Eleanor Roosevelt: An American Journey.* San Diego: San Diego State University Press, 1987. The contributors to this book, a tribute to the accomplishments of Eleanor Roosevelt, include Susan Hartmann and Colleen O'Connor. Chapters deal with ER's efforts in behalf of equal opportunities for women and minorities and of world peace.

Doris Kearns Goodwin. *No Ordinary Time: Franklin and Eleanor Roosevelt and the Home Front in World War II.* New York: Simon and Schuster, 1994. The selection at the beginning of our book on ER's early life comes from this book. The rest of it is just as insightful and well written.

Lewis Gould. *American First Ladies: Their Lives and Their Legacy.* New York: Garland Publishers, 1996. Here are brief biographies of the twentieth century's First Ladies, enabling the reader to find factual and some interpretive information on all of the modern women to hold the place ER used so effectively.

Tamara Hareven. *Eleanor Roosevelt: An American Conscience.* Chicago: Quadrangle Books, 1968. Hareven, whose perceptive comments are used in Parts I and II, presents one of the most complete assessments of ER's life and work available in one volume.

Lorena Hickock. *Reluctant First Lady*. New York: Dodd, Mead, 1962. Hickock, who was ER's close friend, discloses how afraid ER was that being First Lady would require her to end her efforts at social reform. This is the story of how she discovered, to the contrary, that her new forum gave her even greater opportunities than she had previously known.

Eleanor Roosevelt. *The Autobiography of Eleanor Roosevelt*. New York: Harper, 1961. This book combines the various earlier books in which ER had told the stories of her life: *This Is My Story* (1937); *This I Remember* (1949); and *On My Own* (1958); plus some additional material. It is ER's version of the experiences, controversies, and achievements of her long life, published just a year before her death.

———— *It's up to the Women*. New York: Frederick Stokes and Company, 1933. This is ER's first book, and it presents the agenda she has set as First Lady. She will encourage women to take their proper place in American society and politics, and she will be an activist First Lady. It shows what "a progressive woman" thought in 1933.

———— *Ladies of Courage*. New York: Putnam, 1954. Written with Lorena Hickock, this book shows which American women ER admired and why she hoped they could be examples to women of her day. A chapter on ER herself, including her in the list of courageous women, was written solely by Hickock.

———— *The Moral Basis of Democracy*. New York: Howell, Soskin, 1940. This carefully composed book reveals ER's deepest held political beliefs. It may sound in spots quaint today, but she held that the teachings of the Bible and the Founding Fathers were the foundations of any just society.

Susan Ware. *Beyond Suffrage: Women in the New Deal*. Cambridge: Harvard University Press, 1981. Ware gives ER full credit for her part in forwarding the causes and participation of women in this crucial period of U.S. history.

Nancy J. Weiss. *Farewell to the Party of Lincoln*. Princeton: Princeton University Press, 1983. This thoroughly researched study of the social programs of the New Deal explains why black Americans shifted political allegiance from the Republicans of Lincoln to the Democrats of Roosevelt. As Weiss makes clear, ER was more responsible for this change than FDR.

Articles

Blanche Wiesen Cook. "The Real Eleanor." *MS.* (September 1984), pp. 86ff. Cook provides in this recounting of ER's liberal causes her dedication to women's rights and discusses whether she should be considered a feminist.

"Dies vs. Mrs. Roosevelt." *Current History* (January 1940), p. 8. The story of ER's public confrontation with the House UnAmerican Activities Committee and its chairman Congressman Dies over her association with the American Youth Congress, seen by conservatives as a subversive organization.

Elizabeth Janeway. "First Lady of the United Nations." *New York Times Magazine* (October 22, 1950), pp. 12, 61–65. A contemporary assessment of ER's work at the United Nations, including her efforts to draft the Universal Declaration of Human Rights.

Archibald MacLeish. "Tribute to a 'Great American Lady.'" *New York Times Magazine* (November 3, 1963), pp. 17, 118–119. A prominent American author honors ER one year after her death, comparing her to Abigail Adams, wife of the second President.

Kathleen McLaughlin. "First Lady's View of the First-Lady Role." *New York Times Magazine* (January 21, 1940), pp. 3, 20. A good statement of how ER felt, as told to a journalist, about her time as First Lady, written in 1940, after almost eight years in the White House.

Margaret Mead. "Mrs. Roosevelt." *Redbook* (January 1963), p. 120. A tribute by one of the twentieth century's most outstanding women, an anthropologist, about a woman she considered one of the most outstanding.

Eleanor Roosevelt. "In Defense of Curiosity." *Saturday Evening Post* (August 24, 1935), pp. 8–9, 64. One of ER's early essays for the popular press, in which she defends the right of women to keep intellectually alive throughout their lives.

——— "Should Wives Work?" *Good Housekeeping* (December 1937), pp. 28–29, 211–212. Response to a controversial question, in which ER answers that those who are prepared physically and emotionally should do so, and she calls on husbands to be sympathetic and supportive.

——— "The United Nations and You." *Vital Speeches* (May 1, 1946), pp. 444–445. A speech delivered to a high school audience, encouraging youth to appreciate the work of the international organization in which she is about to represent the United States.

——— "What Has Happened to the American Dream?" *Atlantic* (April 1961), pp. 46–50. An essay published eighteen months before her death in which ER once more points to problems in modern society and shows her old spirit of confrontation with them.

——— "Why I Believe in the Youth Congress." *Liberty* (April 20, 1940), pp. 30–32. ER's response to criticism she was receiving for supporting the organization of young liberal Americans who were frightening some of the older members of the establishment, idealistic and headstrong about her convictions as always, even in an election year.

——— "You Can't Pauperize Children." *Ladies Home Journal* (September 1945), pp. 128–129. Still another of ER's causes, published soon after FDR's death, showing that she would continue to be active in social affairs even though she was no longer First Lady.

CREDITS AND ACKNOWLEDGMENTS

Text

Excerpt from "Eleanor Roosevelt at the U.N." by Colleen O'Connor in *Eleanor Roosevelt: An American Journey,* eds. Jess Flemion and Colleen O'Connor (1984), reprinted by permission of San Diego State University Press.

Excerpts from *If You Ask Me* and *It Seems to Me* by Eleanor Roosevelt reprinted by permission of Nancy Roosevelt Ireland.

Excerpt from "Women Have Come a Long Way" by Eleanor Roosevelt in *Harper's Magazine.* Copyright © 1950 by *Harper's Magazine.* All rights reserved. Reproduced from the October issue by special permission.

Photos

INDEX